NOW THE
GOOD NEWS

NOW THE GOOD NEWS

A companion to Luke's Gospel

Andrew Knowles

A LION BOOK

PICTURE CREDITS

Photograghs are reproduced by permission of the
following photographers and agencies:

Barnaby's Picture Library 17, 24, 34, 40, 61
Church Missionary Society, 49
Lion Publishing/David Alexander, 68
Popperfoto, 81
Rex Features, 74
David Simson, 55, 95
A. C. Waltham, 8

Published by
Lion Publishing plc
Icknield Way, Tring, Herts, England
ISBN 0 85648 562 4
Lion Publishing Corporation
10885 Textile Road, Belleville, Michigan 48111, USA
ISBN 0 85648 562 4
Albatross Books
PO Box 320, Sutherland, NSW 2232, Australia
ISBN 0 86760 452 2

First published 1977
This edition 1983
Reprinted 1984

Quotations from the *Good News Bible*, copyright 1966,
1971 and 1976 American Bible Society, published by
Bible Societies/Collins.

Printed in Shen Zhen, China.

Contents

Outsiders' guide to Jesus

1:1-4

Dear Theophilus:
Many people have done their best to write a report of the things that have taken place among us ...

Luke is a doctor. He has a trained eye and a keen mind. He also has a warm love for people.

He wants to tell the whole story of Jesus from the beginning, searching facts, checking dates, ordering events. In this way he hopes to paint a picture of Jesus – a complete picture, a picture for all to see.

Some of Luke's gospel overlaps with the reports of Mark and Matthew. But he has many fresh stories to add.

● He has retraced Jesus' steps.
● He has talked to Jesus' disciples.
● He has met Jesus' family.
● He has listened to many whom Jesus helped and healed.

Luke writes for Theophilus. Theophilus is a man who loves God, but he is a Gentile, a non-Jew, an 'outsider'. Now Luke has good news for Theophilus. **God loves outsiders!**

So here it is: the story of Jesus, told by Luke.

1
GOD
TO THE
RESCUE

Some fear the stars. Some fear disease.
Some fear the emperor. And all fear death . . .

The world is looking for a Saviour.

Waiting for God

1:5-17

During the time when Herod was King of Judaea, there was a priest named Zechariah ... His wife's name was Elizabeth ... They both lived good lives in God's sight ...

The bloody reign of Herod is nearly over. Luke takes us to the very heart of Judaism – the Temple. We meet the very best of Jews – **Zechariah and Elizabeth**.

The priest and his wife are faithful and good. They have been married many years, but have no children. They wonder if God is angry with them ...

One day Zechariah was taking his turn in the daily service ...

This is Zechariah's finest hour. He is leading the Temple service, a chance that comes once in a lifetime. He stands between God and the people, burning the incense, saying the prayers.

The vast crowd is hushed as Zechariah prays: 'Dear God, help your people.'

Suddenly Zechariah sees a most terrifying sight. An angel is standing beside the altar. A mighty messenger of God with a presence that can be felt. 'Zechariah! Your prayer will be answered. Your prayer for the people and your prayer for yourself. God *will* help his people!'

The angel brings astonishing news. Zechariah and Elizabeth will have a son. A son! The dream of every Jewish parent. Every mother and father hoped their child might be the Messiah.

The boy will become an outstanding man of God, a fearless prophet, a signpost pointing to God. He will get people ready for the Messiah. And his name? **John.**

An angel in the Temple? Elizabeth pregnant? A new prophet? God is breaking his long silence. The Baptist is about to be born.

Message for Mary

1:26-38

In the sixth month of Elizabeth's pregnancy God sent the angel Gabriel to a town in Galilee named Nazareth. He had a message for a girl promised in marriage to a man named Joseph ... The girl's name was Mary.

Mary is a young woman. She doesn't usually see angels or hear voices. She's a normal healthy girl looking forward to being married to Joseph.

She is badly frightened by the

arrival of the angel. But he reassures her: **'Don't be afraid, Mary! God has chosen you to have his Son. You must call him Jesus. His name means "God to the rescue." He will be a greater king than David. And his kingdom will last for ever.'**

Mary is very confused. She's engaged to Joseph but they're not living together. They haven't slept together. How can she have a child? It's impossible!

But God can do things which seem impossible. God himself is to be father of the child. He is reaching out to rescue his people.

And what a wonderful reply from Mary. Her reputation is about to be demolished by the local gossips. Her engagement to Joseph may be broken off; she may be divorced or even stoned.

And yet she says:

'I am the Lord's servant. May it happen to me as you have said.'

God's time has come. His place is Nazareth. His person is Mary. His plan is to save mankind.

Messiah's Manifesto

1·46-56

Mary said: 'My heart praises the Lord ...'

Mary has something to sing about! God is using her to keep his promise to Israel.

He had promised Abraham, centuries ago, that he would be the father of a nation. A nation that would bring blessing to the whole world. Now that promise of blessing is coming true through her son.

Mary sings as though it's all cut and dried. When God says something, it's as good as done.

Mary's song is the Messiah's manifesto. The world will be turned upside-down. Proud plans shattered! Tyrants toppled!

Meanwhile the wretched will be rescued, the humble helped and the hungry fed.

Some people worship Mary. She seems closer to God than anyone else. But it's her obedience that makes her close to God. It's her obedience that makes her so happy.

Born in bedlam

2·1-7

Joseph went from the town of Nazareth in Galilee to the town of Bethlehem in Judaea, the birthplace of King David. Joseph went there because he was a descendant of David. He went to register with Mary, who was promised in marriage to him. She was pregnant ...

Nazareth to Bethlehem. Eighty bleak, unwelcome miles.

Every living son of David must report to the family home. But they won't all get in.

Carts and wagons jam the streets. Camels bite, donkeys bray. Women haggle round the fires. Men fight for sleeping space.

The inn is full – of course. And every sheltered corner taken. Joseph and Mary camp in the open square. And there, at an unknown hour, on an unknown night, Mary gives birth.

It's a boy.

While Caesar revels in Rome and Herod rages in Jerusalem, the Son of God is wrapped in cloth and tucked up in a manger. The only cover in the draughty yard.

'No room!' will be the story of his life.

First with the news

2·8-20

There were some shepherds in that part of the country who were spending the night in the fields, taking care of their flocks. An angel of the Lord appeared to them, and the glory of the Lord shone over them. They were terribly afraid, but the angel said to them: 'Don't be afraid! I am here with good news for you, which will bring great joy to all the people.'

Shepherds aren't to be trusted. They don't always stick to their job. They graze their sheep on other men's land. They can't get to synagogue on the Sabbath day.

But it's to shepherds that the good news comes!

'This very night in David's town your Saviour was born – Christ the Lord!'

Christ is Greek for 'Anointed One'. It means the same as Messiah in Hebrew. Jesus is not just another priest or king. He is the Lord's Anointed, the Messiah.

The baby Jesus is being given the highest title known to man.

The world is looking for a Saviour. Some fear the stars. Some fear disease. Some fear the emperor. And all fear death.

The new-born baby is to be a Saviour of Israel. Through him God will offer peace to all men. No wonder the angels are singing!

Welcome and warning

2·21-40

The time came for Joseph and Mary to perform the ceremony of purification, as the Law of Moses commanded.

Jesus is a baby Jew. He must be circumcised when he is one week old. Mary and Joseph take him to the Temple and place him in the arms of Simeon.

Simeon is a good man. He has expected the Messiah for many years.

Now he looks at Jesus and is overjoyed.
But he has hard words for the young family.

● Jesus is God's own light. But many will cling to darkness.
● Jesus will show the world as it is. Men will appear in their true colours. But no-one will thank him for it.
● This baby's birth will force a choice: God or self?

It's 'make-your-mind-up time'.

Teenage Jesus

2·41-52

Every year the parents of Jesus went to Jerusalem ...

The Jesus family go to Jerusalem for passover. Passover is the feast when Jews remember their escape from Egypt.

When Jesus was twelve years old ...

At the age of twelve Jesus becomes a full member of the synagogue – the Jewish church. From now on he is a 'Son of the Law'. He must learn (and keep) the Law for the rest of his life.

This is Jesus' first Passover as an adult. He comes from Galilee in a crowd of pilgrims. A week later, when they are on their way back, Jesus isn't with the rest. The women think he's with the men. The men think he's with the women. That's the trouble when you're twelve.

Mary and Joseph turn back to look for him. It takes a day to return to Jerusalem and another day and a half to find him.

They search the markets and shops, but without success. In despair, they go to the Temple. And there he is!

Deep in conversation with the teachers. Listening and asking questions.

His parents are astonished. The teachers are impressed. This lad from 'up north' certainly knows his stuff.

'My son, why have you done this to us? Your father and I have been terribly worried trying to find you.'

Mary and Joseph can't understand why Jesus is in the Temple. But for Jesus, it's the natural place to be. After all, it's his Father's house.

He's realizing that he's more than 'Son of the Law'. He's 'Son of God'.

Jesus grew ...

Jesus returns to Nazareth. He goes to school and synagogue. He learns Scripture from the rabbi and carpentry from his dad. He walks in the fields and works in the shop. He listens and laughs and loves.

As Luke says:

Jesus grew, both in body and in wisdom, gaining favour with God and men.

2
EARLY DAYS

Twenty years have passed.
Jesus has been in Nazareth working at
a carpenter's bench.
John has been in the desert living in
a holy commune.
Both of them have been in God's classroom.
Now they must make a stand.

Recruiting officer

3.1-20

At that time, the word of God came to John ...

John bursts on the scene like an Old Testament prophet.
'Straighten the bends! Fill in the pot-holes! Flatten the mountains! Here comes God!'
John and Jesus are now about thirty. John is preaching by the River Jordan. He baptizes people, giving them a public bath, if they want to turn to God.

'Turn away from your sins and be baptized ...'

Baptism was more than a wash. It was like drowning. You drowned the past and started again. Clean.
Jews baptized outsiders who wanted to join Israel. But now John is doing something very shocking. **He's baptizing Jews!**
'Don't rely on who you know! Don't say "I'm all right, I come from Abraham". Don't say "I'm all right, I've been 'done'!" What matters is this: **Are you right with God?** You're a fruit tree, and God's the gardener. Is your fruit good or bad? If it's rotten, he'll cut you down!'

Crowds of people came out to John to be baptized by him. 'You snakes!' he said to them. 'Who told you that you could escape from the punishment God is about to send?'

● **God's judgement is like harvest time.** The crop is cut. The stubble is burnt. John looks at the people swarming towards him: like snakes wriggling out of a burning field. Like rats scuttling off a sinking ship.

● **God's judgement is like harvest time.** The wheat is trodden and tossed. The grain falls out, the husk blows off. The wheat is put in the barn. The chaff is put on the fire. That's how it will be when God sorts out his people.

● **God's judgement is like harvest time.** God cares about everything. He cares enough to judge us. He will make sure the good survives; but the bad will be destroyed.
That's good news!

The people asked him, 'What are we to do then?'

When people hear John, they ask questions. 'How can we start to live God's way?' 'What if you're already a twisted tax-man?' 'What if you're already a hard-bitten soldier?'
John gives simple advice.
'If you have spare clothes, share them! If you collect taxes, don't cheat! If you're a soldier, don't bully, and don't be greedy!'

People's hopes began to rise; and they began to wonder ...

The crowds around John grow larger, and more excited. 'He's so strong! He's so straight! Is he ... shhh ... you know who?'
But John puts a stop to the rumour. 'I am not the Messiah. Messiah and I are very different. I baptize with water – river water. He will baptize with

Spirit – and fire! I am the herald but he is the king!'

But John reprimanded Herod, the governor . . .

In the end John spoke too straight for his own good. He said what he thought of Herod. Herod had divorced his wife and married his brother's wife. The affair was a scandal, and John said so!

Herod's answer was just as straight. **He threw John in prison.**

Commissioning Christ

3.21-22

After all the people had been baptized, Jesus also was baptized. While he was praying, heaven was opened, and the Holy Spirit came down upon him in bodily form, like a dove. And a voice came from heaven, 'You are my own dear Son. I am pleased with you.'

One day Jesus comes to be baptized. He stands in the queue with everyone else. When God becomes man, he takes his turn.
   But why? Why does Jesus come to be baptized? He has no sin in his life that needs washing away.
   Jesus wants to belong to his people in every way. Before he can lead them, he must join them on their road. Before he can speak, he must get on their wavelength. So he shares their baptism.
   At this moment, God the Father speaks:

'You are my own dear Son. I am pleased with you.'

The words are echoes of the Old Testament:

● In one of the psalms God says: 'You are my Son, my chosen king.'
● In one of the prophets God says: 'This is my Servant, I am well pleased with him.'

Jesus knows already that he is God's Son and Servant. Now it is time for other people to know. From this moment his life will be out in the open. He will live and die in public.
   The Holy Spirit settles on Jesus. Like a dove fluttering down. Jesus was born by the power of the Holy Spirit. Now he will live and work by the power of the Holy Spirit.
   Jesus is both king and servant. He will rule by serving. He will serve by ruling. All his life he will hold the two together. And in his death he will blend them.

Trial of strength

4·1-13

Jesus returned from the Jordan full of the Holy Spirit and was led by the Spirit into the desert, where he was tempted by the Devil for forty days. In all that time he ate nothing, so that he was hungry when it was over.

The alarm bells are ringing in hell. The Son of God is loose on earth. He must be stopped at all costs.

Jesus paces the wilderness planning his mission. Soon the Devil arrives with some very good ideas. But they all have a catch. His aim is to make Jesus selfish, greedy, or impatient – just for a moment.

The fight is on!

● Round one: 'Help yourself!'

The Devil said to him, 'If you are God's Son, order this stone to turn into bread.'

'Jesus, you're hungry. If you don't eat soon you'll die. What's the use of being God's Son if you're dead?

'Look at those hot brown stones. Don't they look just like fresh bread? Wait a bit. **You can turn them into bread!** Why not help yourself? Just this once?

'No? Well, look at it this way. The world is hungry – right? Starving millions? Swollen bellies and match-stick legs? **If you are the Son of God feed them!** Give them your messiah's feast. They'll expect that from you anyway. Remember Moses fed the people in the wilderness ...

'No? Well, look at it this way. If you are the Son of God you have the power – so why not try it out? Here, where no-one's watching. Just to make sure you can do it ...?'

Jesus answered, 'The scripture says "Man cannot live on bread alone."'

'Satan, you're only half right. I **have** come to fill the hungry, but they need more than bread. They need the bread of life, and that's the word of God.

'**There's more to life than having a full stomach.** I could fill every belly in the world, but men would still be hungry. Hungry for God.'

● Round two: 'King for a day'.

Then the Devil took him up and showed him in a second all the kingdoms of the world. 'I will give you all this power and all this wealth ... if you worship me.'

'Jesus, you're weak. Have you really come to save the world? Don't you realize the world is mine? I own every man, woman and child. They're mine!

'Look here! I'll make you an offer. **You can rule the world if you just bow down to me. That's all you have to do**.

'We'll be partners. You can change the world. Armies and navies, roads and ships, banks and businesses – **all yours** (in exchange for one little bow ...?)

'Look here! You could be the greatest! You could build heaven on earth!

'You can have the go-ahead the moment you kneel to me.'

Jesus answered, 'The scripture says, "Worship the Lord your God and serve only him!"'

'Satan, your power is very great, but I haven't come to join you. I've come to beat you.

'If I am God's Son I must do things God's way, and his way is different from yours. I bow to one person only, and that's God.'

● Round three: 'Flying start'.

Then the devil took him to Jerusalem and set him on the highest point of the Temple, and said to him, 'If you are God's Son, throw yourself down from here . . .'

'Jesus, you're small. You've come to change the world but no-one's ever heard of you! A carpenter's son from Nazareth? You'll never get anywhere!

'Take my tip. Begin in Jerusalem. Begin in the Temple. Begin in a way they'll never forget. **Throw yourself off the top and land in the courtyard. They'll love it!** And you know you'll be all right because you're "God's own dear Son", remember? He won't drop you!'

Jesus answered, 'The scripture says, "Do not put the Lord your God to the test." '

'Satan, I know God won't let me down. I don't need to prove that. **Faith doesn't ask for proof.**

'I'll start from Nazareth and Capernaum and all the little villages. There'll be no short cuts, no cheap tricks, no stunts.

'And Jerusalem? I'll come to Jerusalem soon enough.'

When the Devil finished tempting Jesus in every way, he left him for a while.

Satan has tried everything – including the Bible! But Jesus won't shift.

The Devil goes off to plan his next move. One thing is certain. He'll be back.

Nazareth

4·16-30

Then Jesus went to Nazareth, where he had been brought up, and on the Sabbath he went as usual to the synagogue.

There's a buzz when Jesus comes in. He's the local boy made good. The things they say about him in Capernaum are almost unbelievable. Perhaps he'll preach . . .

Sure enough, the attendant hands the Bible to Jesus. He opens it at the prophet Isaiah, the passage about the Servant of God. Jesus stands up and starts to read:

'The Spirit of the Lord is upon me.

He has sent me to preach good news: good news of freedom, good news of healing, good news of God!'

They listen but they don't hear. They know it by heart. Then Jesus sits down and begins to talk. His first words nearly knock them off their seats.

'This Scripture has just come true!

The Spirit of the Lord is upon me. It's I who bring the good news. Good news day is here! **Good news day is now!**'

They listen but they don't hear. They're busy thinking. What's in it for them? The boy-next-door is Messiah. This'll put Nazareth on the map! They'll be famous! They'll be rich!

But Jesus has more to say.

'Prophets aren't welcome at home. They never have been. They never will be. Elijah helped a widow. But she wasn't a Jew. Elisha cured a leper. But he wasn't a Jew. Must God's messengers always go to foreigners?'

Now they're listening. And they don't like what they hear. This talk of prophets who go to outsiders. They hate it. '**God belongs to the Jews! God belongs to us**!'

Jesus will pay for this. They drag him out of his chair. They drag him out of the synagogue. They drag him out of town.

If he won't live in Nazareth, he won't live anywhere. They head for the cliff. They want to throw him out. Out of their church. Out of their city. Out of their lives.

But Jesus stops. He halts the stampede. He looks them all in the eye. They have never seen such eyes! They falter and draw back. Then he quietly walks through the mob and goes his way.

He never went home again.

Capernaum

4·31-37

Then Jesus went to Capernaum, a town in Galilee, where he taught the people on the Sabbath. They were all amazed at the way he taught, because he spoke with authority.

Happy days for Jesus. Capernaum is at the sea-side, on the shore of Galilee. Here at least Jesus is welcome. He makes the town his base. He teaches in the synagogues.

When Jesus teaches, people listen. His words are alive. While other teachers go round in circles, Jesus talks straight. His words are like well-aimed arrows. They land on target.

But there's more to Jesus than talk. He turns words into deeds. Take the case of the man possessed by an evil spirit. There he is in the synagogue, shouting and screaming . . .

'I know you Jesus! Oh yes, I know all about you. God's agent, come to make trouble!'

Other teachers would have launched into a lot of mumbo-jumbo, waving charms and casting spells. But Jesus simply speaks. **'Muzzle that demon! Come out this minute!'**

The demon throws the man down in a fit of temper. But he comes out of him. Everyone is amazed. Who is this man who tells demons to be off? So far, only the demons know.

A hard day's night

4.38-41

Jesus left the synagogue and went to Simon's house. Simon's mother-in-law was sick ...

It's one of those days! After Jesus has finished at the synagogue, he goes back to lunch with a friend – Simon. He has been teaching all morning. He has dealt with a demon. Now he needs rest.

But there's trouble at home. No food on the table, and mother's taken ill. The old lady has a high fever. She's exhausted. She may die.

Jesus goes over to her bed and **talks to the fever!** Talking to demons is one thing, but talking to fevers is another. Is Satan behind this sickness as well? Jesus tells the fever to go – and it vanishes. Mother-in-law is up and about in no time. In fact she's well enough to serve the meal.

After sunset all who had friends who were sick with various diseases brought them to Jesus; he placed his hands on every one of them and healed them all.

It is the Sabbath. Nobody moves. Nobody works. Nobody plays. Nobody travels.
'On the seventh day of creation, God rested.'
On the seventh day, everyone rests. Until sunset.

And at sunset Capernaum leaps to life! People who haven't lifted a finger all day now shoulder beds and stretchers. They bring all their sick friends to Jesus.

Jesus gives each one the same painstaking attention. He talks to them. He lays hands on them. He heals them all. He works patiently and lovingly. Far into the night.

Moving on

4.42-44

At daybreak Jesus left the town and went off to a lonely place. The people started looking for him, and when they found him, they tried to keep him from leaving.

A long day, and a late night. But Jesus is up early. He needs time to himself. He needs to think. He needs to pray.

'Dear Father,
Things are going very well. I am popular here in Capernaum. I have plenty of work. Enough to keep me busy for months. Shall I stay until every blind man can see, every lame man can walk, and every leper is cured? Is this your will?'

'Dear Son,
Capernaum is just the beginning.
There are other towns and cities,
other districts, other crowds. Healing
is good but it's just a glimpse of my
kingdom, just a taste of my power.
Time is short. You must move on!'

Suddenly Jesus hears footsteps. A
search party has come looking for him.

'Jesus! You gave us a terrible shock.
We thought you'd gone!'

Jesus breaks the news: 'My friends, I
am going. I must preach the good
news of the kingdom in as many
places as possible. That's what God
wants me to do.'

So Jesus leaves Capernaum and takes
to the open road.

3
TEAM CHOICE

Jesus must now form a team,
an inner circle to share his life,
to learn his ways,
to know his mind...

Simon

5·1-11

Jesus got into one of the boats – it belonged to Simon – and asked him to push off a little from the shore.

Simon is in a bad mood. He's been out in the boat all night, and he hasn't caught a thing. All he has to show is a muddy net and a pile of weed. Now there's a whole crowd arriving to give him advice!

Jesus comes to the rescue. 'Simon – may I borrow your boat?'

Simon is tired. He's longing to go home to bed. But he launches the boat, and Jesus sits in it to speak to the crowd.

Simon's mood gets worse. **Why does Jesus have to come this morning? And why does he have to choose his boat?**

Later, Jesus has an idea: 'Simon – push the boat out and try again!'

'Try again?'
Simon comes from Galilee and he

has a temper like a Galilee storm. Is this some sort of joke? What do carpenters know about fishing? It's broad daylight for a start!

'All right – if you say so.'
On the very first cast, they have a catch. And what a catch! The nets are bursting. The boats are sinking. There are fish everywhere!

While the others struggle with the tackle, Simon falls to his knees. Catches like this don't just 'happen'. This is an act of God. 'Lord, you must go away. You shouldn't mix with men like me. You shouldn't be in my boat. You're **holy**! And me – I'm filthy. I'm dirty-minded, foul-mouthed, guilt-ridden . . .'

But Jesus has other ideas: **'Simon – follow me!'**

Jesus gave Simon a new name – Peter. 'Rock!' And he gave him a new job. **Fishing for men!**

Simon left the biggest haul he ever saw. He left the boat, the beach, and all his belongings. From that day on, he was under new management.

Levi

5·27-32

After this, Jesus went out and saw a tax collector named Levi, sitting in his office . . .

Levi is a Customs Officer. A job that

needs a thick skin and a hard heart. A job that makes him the most hated man in Capernaum, without a doubt. He is an official crook. He is barred from law-courts. He is banned from synagogues. He is in the same class as pimps and prostitutes and sneaks.

But he doesn't go through all this

for nothing. With his income, he can afford to be a little unpopular!

From his Customs Office he controls the Galilee border. He collects taxes on imports and exports. He searches baggage. He charges road tax, boat tax, gate tax, trade tax, and transport tax. And he sets the rate of taxation himself, often deciding on the spur of the moment.

When all is safely gathered in, he sends 'enough' to Herod, and keeps the rest for himself.

From his Customs Office he can also see Jesus. The office is on the sea-shore, and Levi has heard many of the Master's sermons. He knows that Jesus is picking a team. He also knows that he won't be in it. He will never be picked for any team. He is an outsider. But he's wrong!

'Levi – follow me!'

For once, Levi asks no questions. He gets up, leaves everything, and follows Jesus. And that takes some doing. The fishermen are only leaving their boats, but Levi is **burning** his.

Herod will never have him back.

The last thing he does before leaving home is to throw a party. The guest list is **A Complete Guide to the Galilean Underworld.** Every rogue in the district is there, elbow to elbow with Jesus.

The Pharisees don't like it. They want their religion kept clean. How can Jesus keep such company? How can he sit in the same room and eat the same food and breathe the same air?

But Jesus has an answer for them: **'Doctors must mix with the sick and I must mix with sinners!'** How else will they hear that God loves them?

So Levi left all: his friends, his foes and his finances.

In return, Jesus gave him a new name – Matthew. 'God-given!' And a new job – **collecting men!**

In the years to come, people would call their dogs 'Caesar' and their sons 'Matthew'. Just one of the changes Jesus makes!

Inner circle

6·12-16

At that time, Jesus went up a hill to pray, and spent the whole night there praying to God. When day came, he called his disciples to him and chose twelve of them, whom he named apostles ...

Jesus is a strategist. He sees the end from the beginning. He knows he

must now form a team: an inner circle to share his life, to learn his ways, to know his mind.

Jesus prays all night about the crucial choice: 'Father, I need close friends. Men of good heart, willing to learn, ready to work. Men I can send out as you have sent me. Help me to choose wisely.'

And so Jesus calls twelve disciples. The number is no accident. They are to be the nucleus of the New Israel, the foundation stones of the church.

Jesus chooses quite ordinary men. They come from various walks of life. Some of them are middle class. Several of them are fishermen. They have differing temperaments and they disagree about politics!

TWELVE DISCIPLES

PETER is the natural leader, and quickly becomes the spokesman! He is warm-hearted and impetuous.

ANDREW is a fisherman, like his brother Peter. He has a quiet manner and makes friends easily.

JAMES and **JOHN** are brothers, and they, too, are fishers. They are so ambitious and explosive that Jesus calls them 'Sons of Thunder'!

PHILIP and **BARTHOLOMEW** already know each other. They both come from Galilee.

MATTHEW is a tough, well-educated character. He has trained and worked as a tax-collector.

THOMAS is a twin. He is doggedly honest, and people respect him for it.

SIMON is a fanatical nationalist. He belongs to the underground movement against the Romans.

JUDAS ISCARIOT is very keen, and appears responsible. The group appoint him Treasurer.

JUDAS and another **JAMES** make up the number, but we know little more than their names.

For three hectic years these men will be with Jesus, sharing the joys and sorrows of the teacher from Nazareth. They will listen and learn. They will travel and teach.
  Slowly but surely they will be grafted into the life of God.
  At the end, one of them will betray Jesus. And the rest will desert him.

New light

9·28-36

Jesus took Peter, John and James with him and went up a hill to pray. While he was praying, his face changed its appearance, and his clothes became dazzling white. Suddenly two men were there talking with him.

The track leads up a hill. Jesus goes ahead. Peter, John and James trek behind. They are climbing Mount Hermon – to pray.
  Jesus often goes off to pray. Usually he goes by himself. But today he takes the in-group with him. They may be there all night.
  Suddenly, a bright light shines all round them. The light is coming from Jesus! His face – his clothes – dazzling white!
  As they look, he is joined by two men, Moses and Elijah. Moses the Law-giver. Elijah the Prophet. The Best of the Old Testament.
  Moses and Elijah talk to Jesus.

Where will he go from here? Which is his way out? Moses made his way out through the Red Sea. Elijah made his way out by fiery chariot. And Jesus?

For Jesus there is no easy way out. His road leads to Jerusalem. His ladder to heaven is a wooden cross.

Peter interrupts. 'Master, this is great! We never realized! I mean – we've never seen you like this before! Let's stay here for ever. We'll soon make shelters. It won't take long . . .'

As he talks, a bright cloud hides Jesus and the others. And God speaks to the disciples:

'This is my Son . . . listen to him!'

God has spoken through the Law. God has spoken through the Prophets. **Now God speaks through his Son!**

The cloud fades. The light dies away. And there stands Jesus. No Moses. No Elijah. Only Jesus.

The track leads down the hill. Jesus goes ahead. The disciples trek behind. He is going to Jerusalem – to die.

Samaritan road

9·51-56

As the time drew near when Jesus would be taken up to heaven, he made up his mind and set out on his way to Jerusalem.

Jesus leaves the north for the last time. From now on his road goes south – to Jerusalem.

Jerusalem. The city that kills God's prophets. The city that throws rocks at his messengers. It's a journey to death, and Jesus knows it. But his mind is made up.

The road goes through enemy territory – Samaria. The Samaritans have a temple of their own. They hate Jewish pilgrims taking a short cut across their land to get to the Temple in Jerusalem. Sometimes they even attack the travellers.

However, the Samaritans like Jesus. And Jesus has a lot of time for them.

Soon he will tell a story of a **good** Samaritan. Soon he will cure ten lepers, and the only one who bothers to thank him will be a Samaritan.

Jesus wants to stay the night in a village. He sends a message that he is coming. But when they hear where he is going, they slam the doors in his face. If Jesus was coming to their temple, they might give him a bed.

But they hear he is on his way to Jerusalem . . . Once again, there is 'no room' for Jesus.

James and John are wild! How dare the Samaritans lock out their master? 'Lord, say the word, and we'll call fire from heaven to destroy the whole village. That'll teach them manners!'

James and John have Elijah on the brain – ever since they saw him on the mountain. They remember how Elijah called fire from heaven to scorch two captains and their servants who came to arrest him. They believe Jesus can do the same. Jesus has to cool them down. 'Elijah called down fire from heaven because he didn't know any better. **But I tell you to love your enemies!'**

And so they move on to another village. If they would follow Jesus, they must see people with his eyes. They must love with his love. They must do things his way.

All or nothing

9·57-62

As they went on their way, a man said to Jesus, 'I will follow you wherever you go.'

Many people wanted to join Jesus. Some volunteered. Others were called. Either way, Jesus told them what it would cost them to go with him. And he told them straight!

● **No home.** One man said: **'I will follow you wherever you go.'** But Jesus said: 'Think again!

'Do you know what you're saying? Most people have a home to go to. Even hunted animals have bolt-holes and dens. Birds can shelter in trees. But if you follow me, you'll have no home, no bolt-hole, no shelter. The only place I'll lie down will be a wooden cross.'

● **No delay.** Another man said: **'Sir, first let me go back and bury my father.'** But Jesus said: 'Think again!

'I know you love your father. I know you want to be a good son. But isn't that just an excuse? He may not die for many years yet! My work is urgent. So follow me now – or never.'

● **No regrets.** Another man said: **'I will follow you, sir; but first let me go and say goodbye to my family.'** But Jesus said: 'Think again!

'If you come with me you must leave the old ways. It's like ploughing. You can't look in front of you and behind you at the same time. You must leave the past – and follow me!'

Today's advertisers put the cost in small print. Not so Jesus. He puts his price in the headlines:

TO FOLLOW ME WILL COST YOU – YOUR LIFE!

No rights reserved

14.25-33

Once when large crowds of people were going along with Jesus, he turned and said to them, 'Whoever comes to me cannot be my disciple unless he loves me more than he loves his father and and his mother, his wife and his children, his brothers and his sisters, and himself as well. Whoever does not carry his own cross and come after me cannot be my disciple ... None of you can be my disciple unless he gives up everything he has.'

Every day the crowd gets bigger. Galilee votes Jesus 'The Greatest'. They swing along the road behind him, coining slogans, singing songs. **But it's quite possible to follow Jesus without realizing where he's going.**

Jesus has to round on them and make himself clear. 'Listen everybody! This isn't a holiday outing! I don't want spectators or well-wishers. **I want disciples!**'

Jesus outlines the terms of the contract:

● **Jesus comes before family**
Jesus before mother and father. Jesus before wife and children. Jesus before brothers and sisters. Jesus before self!

All these relationships are close. All these relationships are good. But when it comes to the choice, a disciple must prefer Jesus.

● **Jesus comes before comfort**
A disciple must go the same way as Jesus. He may be teased, taunted or tortured, but he mustn't protect or defend himself. He must swim against the tide of popular opinion. He must ignore the crowd and follow the master.

And when the leader suffers, the follower can't ask for less.

● **Jesus comes before self**
A disciple must sign away all rights to himself. His wealth is no longer his own. His ambitions no longer matter. His life now belongs to Christ.

Jesus says: 'Think carefully about these terms. You think before you build a tower. You think before you start a war. **So think before you follow me!**'

Travelling light

10·1-9

After this the Lord chose another seventy-two men and sent them out, two by two, to go ahead of him to every town and place where he himself was about to go.

The disciples must travel light. No money. No spares. No delays. They must go where they are told, eat what they're given, and stay where they're welcome. They take with them nothing but 'Peace'.

Jesus looks at them. They are raw recruits. They stand as much chance as a lamb in a wolf-pack. But God is on their side. And they must trust him.

The mission is urgent. Like harvest time. The workers must go all out when the crop's ready and the weather's fine. Harvest time doesn't last for ever.

Israel is ripe! God is the owner of the harvest. The disciples are the workers. And time is short.

Opportunity knocks!

10·10-16

But whenever you go into a town and are not welcomed, go out into the streets and say, 'Even the dust from your town that sticks to our feet we wipe off against you. But remember that the kingdom of God has come near you!' I assure you that on Judgement Day God will show more mercy to Sodom than to that town!

The disciples take God's kingdom wherever they go. They are his reps. His agents. Whenever they speak they must tell of God. Wherever they work they must heal and help. Wherever they stay they must bring his peace.

But what if the people don't want to know? Jesus says God's judgement on them will be terrible.

Chorazin, Bethsaida, Capernaum, three thriving centres. But they have rejected God's Son. They have heard his words, seen his deeds, and turned away! Now God will reject them. He will be tougher on them than he was on Sodom, because Sodom never had their chance. Sodom never saw Jesus.

When a town rejects God's messengers, God's messengers must reject that town. They must shake the dust off their shoes as if they are leaving unholy ground.

Opportunity has knocked and they have locked their doors. The choice was theirs. Chorazin, Bethsaida, Capernaum. Three thriving centres.

Today Chorazin and Capernaum are in ruins. And Bethsaida? We can't even find where it was!

Success

10·17-20

The seventy-two men came back in great joy. 'Lord,' they said, 'even the demons obeyed us when we gave them a command in your name!' Jesus answered them, 'I saw Satan fall like lightning from heaven.'

Jesus means 'God to the Rescue'. And the disciples find that it's true. As they preach in the name of Jesus, they find they have power: power to expel demons.

They return with joy! And Jesus too is joyful:

'I saw Satan fall like lightning from heaven'.

Satan is an accuser. He informs God of all the wrong we have done. He presses hard for justice – without mercy. He wants to make sure we get what we deserve – death.

Satan is a liar. He tells us lies about God. He tells God lies about us. **But now Satan is on the way out.**

The walls of his kingdom are being broken down. Tidal waves of truth and life are crashing over his empire. The disciples are delighted. But Jesus warns them not to grow proud:

'You are channels for God's power. Nothing can stand in his way. You can walk on snakes, tread on scorpions, throw out demons. But Satan can do the same. And if you get proud, you'll be no better than him. No. There is only one thing to be glad about: **your names are written in heaven!**

Satan has been thrown out and you have been welcomed in.'

4
TOPSY-TURVY
TEACHING

Jesus is full of surprises.
Often he says the opposite of what we expect.
He moves things back-to-front,
he turns them upside-down.

But when his teaching **seems** topsy-turvy
remember one thing ...
it's Jesus who is right way up

Life is death

12·33-34

Jesus said: **'Sell all your belongings and give the money to the poor. Provide for yourselves purses that don't wear out, and save your riches in heaven, where they will never decrease, because no thief can get to them, and no moth can destroy them. For your heart will always be where your riches are.'**

There's nothing wrong with money. It's loving money that's wrong. We must possess our belongings – not worship them!

Jesus says: **'Your heart will always be where your riches are.'**

Our standard of living isn't anything to do with our wallet. It's to do with

our **heart**. Jesus said that two thousand years ago. But we still don't hear. We still assess people by what they earn. A business man is good. A beggar is bad.

But that's not how God sees it. He looks for spiritual riches. He wants us to let go of our worldly wealth, and invest our lives with him in heaven.

Jesus says: 'Look at it this way. Moths will eat your clothes, rust will eat your car, time will eat your health, inflation will eat your savings, death will eat your body – and what then? If that was your life, then you wasted it!'

Jesus urges us to keep our hearts in heaven: to hold money lightly; to give help freely; to live life boldly. Then we will have true wealth. Men can't steal it; death can't snatch it.

That wealth is eternal life.

Death is life

9·23-25

Jesus said: **'If anyone wants to come with me, he must forget self, take up his cross every day, and follow me. For whoever wants to save his own life will lose it; but whoever loses his life for my sake will save it.'**

The world says, 'Never say die.' Jesus says, 'You *must* die!'

Imagine a table. Put on the table all the things you want to give to God. Your time. Your money. Your home. Your friends. Your job. Your pastimes. You need a bigger table! You seem to be giving everything to God.

But the one thing God wants is still missing. **He wants you.** You must clamber on the table yourself. But the world says, 'Never say die.'

The world calls us to a standard of

living: 'Help yourself!' 'Prove yourself!' 'Spoil yourself!' 'You **deserve** a portable television. A holiday with a difference. A fitted kitchen. A new L.P.'

'Never mind that others are hungry. Never mind that others are naked. Never mind that others are lonely. You're only young once. Enjoy it! Get out and **live**!'

But Jesus says, 'You must **die**.'

If anyone wants to come with me, he must forget self, take up his cross every day, and follow me.

'If anyone wants to come my way, he must shoulder the cross, and walk through the mob, every day of his life. If you won't be seen dead with me, you certainly won't be seen alive with me.'

We'll do anything rather than die. We'll give money. We'll remain single. We may even become missionaries! But we don't want to die.

But Jesus says: 'Why are you saving your life? What are you saving it **for**? You have one life to **spend**. So why save it?

'You must spend each day as it comes. It is date-stamped. It won't keep! If you try to save your life, keep it in cotton-wool, never take a knock, never take a risk, you'll lose it!

'But if you spend your life on me, if you throw in your life with mine, then you'll live! And that's real life.'

Rich is poor

12·13-21

A man in the crowd said to Jesus, 'Teacher, tell my brother to divide with me the property our father left us.' Jesus answered him, 'My friend, who gave me the right to judge or to divide the property between you two?' And he went on to say to them all, 'Watch out and guard yourselves from every kind of greed; because a person's true life is not made up of the things he owns, no matter how rich he may be.'

Someone is worried about his standard of living. He's afraid he won't have his fair share. But he gets little sympathy from Jesus! In fact Jesus tells a story to make a rich man think twice.

'There was once a rich man who had a good year on the farm. It was the harvest of a lifetime. He had so much grain he didn't know where to store it all. It was really quite worrying. One night he lay in bed thinking. And he had an idea.

' "Of course! I'll pull down the old barns and build new ones. Bigger ones. Then, with all my grain under cover, I can retire. I'll take it nice and easy. Eat well. Sleep well. Drink plenty. Catch up with old friends ... I can hardly wait for morning!"

'But God said to the man: 'You're a fool! A complete and utter fool! You won't be needing those barns because tonight you die. And what's the use of your sweet dreams then?" '

Jesus says: 'The only wealth that lasts is spiritual. There's more to life than feeding your stomach and clothing your body. The most important thing in life is to know God. That's real life and real wealth.'

Poor is rich

21.1-4

Jesus looked round and saw rich men dropping their gifts in the Temple treasury, and he also saw a very poor widow dropping in two little copper coins ...

In the Temple are thirteen containers shaped like upside-down trumpets. Jesus and his disciples sit watching the money flowing in. It comes in such quantities that the Temple must be worth millions! And giving to the Temple has become quite a spectator sport!

Jesus notices a woman in the crowd. He can tell by her clothes that she's a widow. Widows have no income, and few jobs are open to them. As he watches, she drops two copper coins into one of the trumpets. Two coppers – known as 'thin'uns'. The smallest donation allowed. Less would be an insult! And so she goes on her way.

Jesus says to his disciples: 'That widow has just put in more than all the rest put together! The others are putting in their spare cash. **But she has just thrown in her life.'**

We have a loving and generous God. He has given us a magnificent creation – free of charge. He has given us intricate bodies and minds – free of charge. He has given us families and friends – free of charge.

The sun will rise tomorrow. The air will be fresh. The crops will grow. But there's no invoice. **It's free!**

More than that. **God has saved us.** He has bought us out of slavery – he has made the most expensive purchase in history. And the price? The life of his Son! But there's no invoice. **It's free!**

If God has given so generously to us, shouldn't we give generously to him? Not because we have to, but because we **want** to?

God loves happy givers. Laughing Policeman-type givers! The man who gives generously to God is the happiest man in town.

Last is first

9·46-48

An argument broke out among the disciples as to which one of them was the greatest. Jesus knew what they were thinking, so he took a child, stood him by his side, and said to them, 'Whoever welcomes this child in my name, welcomes me; and whoever welcomes me, also welcomes the one who sent me.'

The disciples have been busy. They are carving up the kingdom of God. Twelve delicious slices! But who will have the largest? Peter, James and John seem to be favourites. The others are jealous and critical.

Then Jesus shows them a child.

'You want to know who's great in the kingdom? Look at this child! He has no power, no prestige. He can't pay you or promote you. If you spend your life serving people like this for my sake, then you'll be great in God's reckoning.'

Most of us will serve so long as someone is watching and the money's right. **Jesus says we must serve for no other reason than love for him.**

That's great!

First is last

22·24-27

An argument broke out among the disciples as to which one of them should be thought of as the greatest ...

It's the night of Jesus's arrest. The disciples are with him at table. And the old argument flares up again ...

'Here we are on the threshold of power! Who's to be Prime Minister? Who's to be Secretary of State?'

It's agony for Jesus to hear them. To think they've come so far, and learnt so little. He interrupts them:

'It's not that sort of kingdom! In this world, power is the name of the game The "Great" are those who dominate and dictate, who lean on people and throw their weight around. But in my kingdom the "Friend of the People" isn't the President. The "Friend of the People" is the servant.

'In this world you serve for what you can get out of it. In my kingdom your joy is what you can put into it.'

Jesus comes as a servant. He puts his life at our disposal. Christian leadership means dying to self for the sake of others.

Just like Jesus.

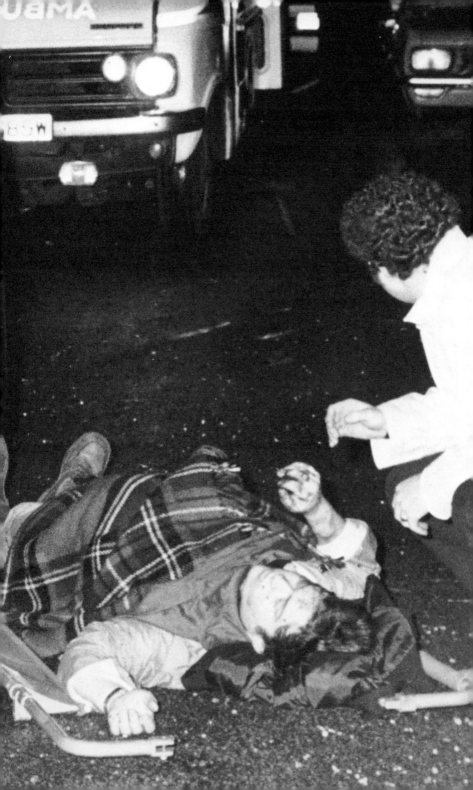

5
SHOCKING STORIES

Jesus tells stories to shock!

To us they seem 'good' stories.
Nice to tell children at bedtime.
But to some who heard them
they were horror stories!

These were never meant for children.

Spot the neighbour

10.25-37

A teacher of the Law came up and tried to trap Jesus. 'Teacher,' he asked, 'what must I do to receive eternal life?' Jesus answered him, 'What do the Scriptures say? How do you interpret them?' The man answered, ' "Love the Lord your God with all your heart, with all your soul, with all your strength, and with all your mind"; and, "Love your neighbour as you love yourself." ' 'You are right,' Jesus replied; 'do this and you will live.'

But the teacher of the Law wanted to justify himself, so he asked Jesus, 'Who is my neighbour?'

The lawyer has a problem. He knows where to start loving, but he can't decide where to stop! He knows he must love God and his neighbour. But who is his neighbour?

To help him, Jesus tells a story:

'A man was on the deadly road to Jericho. Seventeen miles of danger. Narrow, twisting, overhung, and dropping steeply all the way. A sitting target for muggers . . . And he **was** mugged! Ambushed, beaten, robbed, and left for dead.

'First on the scene was a priest. A man who believed in love. Surely he would help. But no. He was on his way to work. He needed clean hands for the Temple. Touching a corpse would set him back a week! He crossed the road and walked on by, admiring the vultures . . .

'Then round the bend came a Levite. The next best thing to a priest. He saw the wounded man, and took a closer look. But then he hurried away. Perhaps he was scared of blood. Perhaps he suspected a trick. Perhaps he simply didn't care . . .

'The day wore on. The man's life began to ebb away. And then, in the dusk, a third traveller came by. But it was only a Samaritan. He would do the inevitable – spit on the Jew and push off . . .

'Wrong!

'In an instant, the Samaritan was off his donkey. He knelt by the poor man's side; he cleaned and gently covered his wounds; he lifted him carefully on to his beast.

'By nightfall they were both in a cosy inn. And the Samaritan stayed with the patient till dawn. The following day, he left. But not before paying for the Jew to stay for several weeks to come!'

Jesus turns to the lawyer and smiles. 'Well now – spot the neighbour!'

When do we stop loving? Where do we draw the line? Jesus says: 'There is no line. Your neighbour is whoever you can help. And let that help be generous.'

Beggars' banquet

14·15–24

When one of the men sitting at table heard this, he said to Jesus, 'How happy are those who will sit down at the feast in the Kingdom of God!' Jesus said to him, 'There was once a man who was giving a great feast to which he invited many people . . .'

Jesus is feasting with Pharisees. During the evening, someone says: 'Won't it be nice when we all sit down to dine in heaven?' He's obviously expecting to be there! But Jesus has different ideas. He tells them a story:

'There was once a man who gave a feast. He invited hundreds of people. In fact he invited them twice! First an "early warning", to tell them the dinner was planned. Then a message on the day to say that the food was ready.

'And guess what? Nobody came. **Nobody!**

'One after another they sent their excuses:

● "Sorry – I've just bought a field. I must go and inspect it."

● "Sorry – I've just bought some oxen. I must go and try them out."

● "Sorry – I've just got married. I must stay with my wife."

'The master was furious! Their excuses were utterly flimsy. The truth was that nobody wanted to come. Nobody buys a field without seeing it first. Nobody buys ten oxen without trying them first. And as for being married – that doesn't stop you eating! He could bring his wife with him.

'Then the master had an idea. He sent his servant to search the back streets, to bring in the poor, to lead in the blind, to carry in the cripples – and still there was room!

'So the master sent his servant out of town to the country roads and lanes, the hedges and ditches, where tramps doss down, where lepers hide.

' "Force them to come in!" shouted the master. "I won't take 'No' for an answer. I want my house to be full. If my friends won't come, I'll invite strangers!"

'What a scene! Hundreds of down-and-outs having the feast of a lifetime. A Beggars' Banquet. And the happiest man there was the master.'

The Pharisees don't like the story. The master is God. The guests who make excuses are Jews. They know they're being got at!

Jesus is warning of surprises at the heavenly banquet. Many who claim to know God will be missing. Many sinners and outsiders will be there.

And the message for us? **Heaven is like a feast! God is a master who longs for a full house. His table is 'Free for all'. And we must be sure to drop everything – and come!**

One in a hundred

15·1-7

One day when many tax collectors and other outcasts came to listen to Jesus, the Pharisees and the teachers of the Law started grumbling, 'This man welcomes outcasts and even eats with them!' So Jesus told them this parable: 'Suppose one of you has a hundred sheep and loses one of them ...'

Pharisees keep themselves to themselves. They don't want other people's sins rubbing off on them. **They can't understand Jesus.** He keeps company with all and sundry. Every day they see shifty characters going to him. Men and women with suspect morals and shady jobs, going to see Jesus – and staying to dinner! So Jesus tells the Pharisees a story:

'A man with a hundred sheep discovers that one is missing. So, of course, he leaves the ninety-nine grazing, and goes in search of the stray.

'When he finds it lying in a ditch or stuck on a ledge, he's overjoyed! He carries it home on his shoulders. He calls the neighbours to share his delight.

'And believe me, God is like that shepherd. He summons the angels in heaven to rejoice with him when one in a hundred is found and brought home.'

God is like a shepherd. He wants to do everything for his people. When a person is lost, in trouble, or out of touch, God will spare no effort to come and help.

The Pharisees think that God wants all sinners dead. They couldn't be more wrong.

Jesus says: 'God wants all sinners alive! Alive and well and safely home! That's what gives God joy.'

Rich man, poor man

16·19-31

There was once a rich man who dressed in the most expensive clothes and lived in great luxury every day. There was also a poor man, named Lazarus ...

'Rich Man has everything. A large house with lavish furnishings. A wardrobe full of sumptuous clothes. And as for food: he has a late breakfast, an early lunch, afternoon tea, and an evening banquet.

'At his back door, lies Poor Man. He's a beggar and a cripple. He's dumped there every day. He eats any crumbs which are swept out of Rich Man's house. He's a bundle of rags and bones. His name is Lazarus. His

best friends are dogs. **Poor Man has
nothing.**

'One day they both die.

'The whole town stops work for
Rich Man's funeral. A large crowd
watches his gold coffin go by. Hired
men weep. Meanwhile, the dustman
has picked up Poor Man's body – and
thrown it on the garbage tip.

'The scene changes. And what a
change.

'We're in for a shock. Poor Man has
gone to heaven! Rich Man has gone to
hell!

'Rich Man can't believe his eyes.
There's Lazarus, sitting beside
Abraham. Abraham! The Father of the
Jews! What's the beggar doing in the
seat of honour while he's in hottest
hell?

'He calls out: "Father Abraham!
Send that beggar down here with a
drop of water! I'm absolutely
parched!"

'But Abraham replies: "No way!
There's a great gap between heaven
and hell so that no-one can cross after
death."

'Then Rich Man has a thought
which makes his agony ten times
worse. "My brothers! What about my
five brothers? They're still alive!

They're eating and drinking without a
thought for others. They'll end up here
with me, unless I can warn them . . .
Father Abraham! Send the beggar to
warn my brothers!"

'But Abraham says: "They've
already been warned. Moses warned
them. The Prophets warned them.
They've got their Bibles . . ."

'Rich Man cries out: "But that's no
good. They need a real shock. Send
Lazarus to frighten them. That'll make
them think!"

'Abraham answers: "Miracles never
change anybody. If they don't take
notice of God's messengers, they
certainly won't listen to a ghost!" '

**Jesus tells the story as a warning.
Now is the time to live for God. You
will never be forced to believe. You
will never be forced to do good.**

But after death comes judgement.

We are the five brothers. We have
the good news of Jesus. If we don't
listen to him, then nothing else will
persuade us.

Are we waiting for further
information? Writing in the sky? A
blinding flash? It will never come!

We must decide from what we
already know.

And we must decide now.

Welcome home

15·11-32

**Jesus went on to say, 'There was once a
man who had two sons. The younger
one said to him, "Father, give me my
share of the property now."**

'**A man had two sons and he loved
them both.** But they wanted his
money, and they wished he was dead.
The elder son decided to wait for the
money at home. But the younger son
asked for his share in cash, and left.

'At first all was well. He went as far
from home as possible, and started to

spend. He went out with lots of girls, danced all night and slept all day. But the money ran out!

'As his cash disappeared, so did his friends. All of a sudden he was alone. And he had to get a job – any job.

'He ended up working as a pig-man for a Gentile. The worst job on earth for a Jew, because Jews never touch pork. The boy had to feed the pigs. But nobody fed him.

'Alone in the sty, he began to think. He had set out to be free, and ended up a slave. What was he worth now? No cash, no smart suit, no girls to go out with. Well, he was still his father's son and nothing could change that.

'Suddenly he wasn't just hungry. He was home-sick! He got to his feet and started for home. As he limped the long miles in his bare feet he made up a short speech:

'Father, I have sinned against God and against you. I am no longer fit to be called your son; treat me as one of your hired workers.'

'Back home, the father was on the roof-top watching. As soon as his son appeared on the horizon, he ran out to meet him. The son began to blurt out his little speech:

'Father, I have sinned against God and against you. I am no longer fit ...'

'The father's face was glowing, but not with anger. He was overjoyed! He called to the servants: **"Bring the best robe! Fetch a ring! Find some shoes! He's alive! He's home!"**

'They killed the prize calf. The whole household started feasting. But one person was missing – the elder brother. He was still working in the fields, being a good son.

'When he arrived home that evening, the house was a blaze of lights. He could hear music and laughter and dancing! He looked again at the number on the gate. Yes – it was his father's house all right. Had they all gone mad? The servant opened the door.

' "What's all the noise about?" asked the elder brother. "The young master has come home, sir. Your father has killed the prize calf!"

' **"So he's come home has he? Well if he's in the house, I'll stay out here. And if he stays, I go!"**

'The father came out and pleaded with him. But the elder son was full of righteous anger: "Look Dad, I've slaved away all these years doing whatever you say and being a good boy. And you never gave me so much as a goat to share with a few friends. Then that lay-about comes home. Your so-called son who has wasted half your money. And you kill the prize calf!"

'But the father said:

'My Son! You are always here with me, and everything I have is yours ...'

'The elder son had been at home all the time. He had enjoyed his father's love and care. In fact he had taken it for granted.

'But we had to celebrate and be happy, because your brother was dead, but now he is alive; he was lost, but now he has been found.'

What's so shocking? The younger son is a sinner who has strayed from God. But when he turns for home, God comes running to meet him!

The elder son is a self-righteous Pharisee. He wants to keep all sinners out of heaven. He disowns people and is quick to think the worst of them.

If we don't rejoice when sinners repent, then we don't know God very well.

6
POWERFUL
PRAYERS

The disciples wish they could pray like
Jesus. They **say** their prayers. But they
don't always **mean** them ...

God's a dad

11·1-2

One day Jesus was praying in a certain place. When he had finished, one of his disciples said to him, 'Lord, teach us to pray ...'

The disciples are hanging about. Waiting for Jesus – again. **He is praying – again!** The disciples wish they could pray like Jesus. They **say** their prayers. But they don't always **mean** them.

When Jesus is finished, they pluck up courage to ask him: 'Lord – give us a prayer. John gave his disciples a prayer. What about one for us?'

Jesus agrees.

He sits down, and they gather round.

'Well it's like this. When you pray, when you approach almighty, everlasting, all-seeing, all-knowing God, this is what you should say ...'

This is the moment they've been waiting for. They're all ears. And then comes the bombshell. Jesus begins:

'Dear Dad ...'

The disciples are shocked and dazed. Jesus has just uttered a blasphemy. No-one has ever **dared** call God 'Daddy' before. In fact no-one has dared to call God **anything**. His name is too holy to be touched by human lips.

But this is Jesus' secret. When he prays, he is talking to his Father. No wonder he finds so much to talk about. No wonder he loves to pray.

And that's not all. Jesus invites us to come to God in the same way. We are members of God's family, brothers and sisters of Jesus, and children of God.

And so we can all pray: **'Our Father ...'**

God rules – OK

11·2-4

Jesus said to them, 'When you pray, say this: "Father: May your holy name be honoured; may your kingdom come. Give us day by day the food we need. Forgive us our sins, for we forgive everyone who does us wrong. And do not bring us to hard testing."'

Jesus doesn't rush into prayer with a shopping list of man's needs. He begins with God.

● **'May your holy name be honoured.** May people respect you, Creator Lord. May they worship you whole-heartedly, and speak of you reverently.'

● **'May your kingdom come.** Father, you long to rule. But you want the

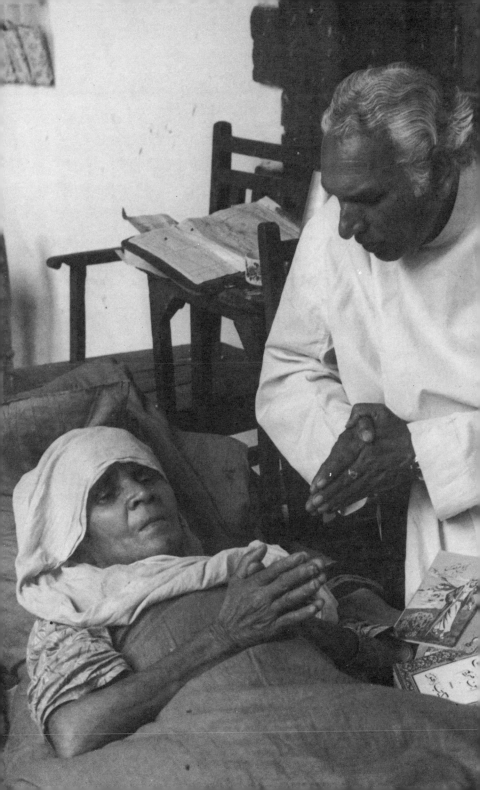

world to **choose** you. May your love spread everywhere. May more and more men and women make you King of their lives.'

And then Jesus lists our needs.

● **'Give us day by day the food we need.** Father, we remember the Israelites in the wilderness. Every morning they picked up enough food for the day. Give us today enough for today. No greed, no grabbing, no hoarding. Just **enough**. And help us to trust you for tomorrow when it comes.'

● **'Forgive us our sins, for we forgive everyone who does us wrong.'** 'Father, please forgive and forget the wrong things we've done. The times we've let you down. The times we've defied you. Let us be friends with you again. And help us to treat others in the same way. Always ready to say "Sorry" – and mean it. Always quick to say "That's all right – forget it." And mean it!'

● **'And do not bring us to hard testing.** Father, serving you is going to get harder. Satan wants to see us dead. Some time there's going to be a pitched battle. Father, may it never be too much for us! You alone can help.'

No need to nag

11·5-13

And Jesus said to his disciples, 'Suppose one of you should go to a friend's house at midnight and say to him, "Friend, let me borrow three loaves of bread ..."'

Jesus tells a story: 'Imagine it's late – very late. You're about to switch out the light and go to sleep, when there's a knock at the door. It's a friend. He's been overtaken by nightfall and needs bed and breakfast. But you haven't a scrap of food in the house!

'You go next door. They've always got bread. The house is in darkness. You knock gently.

'Nothing happens. You knock louder. A sleepy voice calls out "Go away!" You shout back "It's me! I say, someone's arrived unexpectedly. Can you lend me some bread?"

'The voice comes back, "No! We're all in bed. My wife is tired. The baby's only just gone to sleep. Go away!"

'But you knock again. And you shout again. And you go on knocking and shouting, until in the end he gives in. He gets out of bed and gives you all the food you want. Not because he loves you, but because he wants to get rid of you.'

Jesus goes on: **'The point is this. Your neighbour will answer you in the end because you threaten to batter down the door. But God isn't like that. He isn't reluctant. He isn't asleep. In fact he looks forward to hearing from you!**

'So knock! And ask! God's not a sleepy neighbour. He's a loving father.'

Keep going

18·1-8

Then Jesus told his disciples a parable to teach them that they should always pray and never become discouraged. 'In a certain town there was a judge who neither feared God nor respected man. And there was a widow in that same town who kept coming to him and pleading for her rights ...'

Jesus is telling another story about prayer.

'There was once a crooked judge. A pig with a wig! He was only in it for the money. He didn't care what anyone said. He certainly didn't care about God.

'In his town there was a widow. She kept coming to the judge about her case. She said someone owed her some money.

'Well, of course, the judge didn't care. The widow had no powerful friends, no cash for bribes. And anyway, he didn't fancy her! So he told her to go away.

'But she kept coming. She came every day. First thing in the morning when he arrived at court, there she was. Nag, nag, nag! She didn't even stop for lunch! And she stayed all day.

'Before long he began to dread saying "Next case!" because it might be her. In the end he couldn't stand it any longer. He gave in.

' "All right Madam, you win. I don't know whether you're right or wrong, and I don't care. But I'll be a nervous wreck if you go on any longer. You're giving me bags under the eyes! Have whatever you want!" '

Jesus says: **'If a bent judge will give in to a poor widow simply because she nags him, how much more will God, the perfect judge, hear you when you pray!'**

So ask God for the things you need. And never give up!

Be yourself

18·9-14

Jesus also told this parable to people who were sure of their own goodness and despised everybody else. 'Once there were two men who went up to the Temple to pray: one was a Pharisee, the other a tax collector.'

'Pharisee strides into the Temple. He comes three times a day. They know him well.

'He finds a nice clear space where people can get a good view of him and begins to pray.

' "Here I am, God. Your favourite person! Thank you that I am so good. I starve on Monday and Thursday. I give away a tenth of all my goods. I'm

fair, I'm honest, I'm moral. Thank you
that I'm not a Gentile, or a Samaritan,
or a leper, or a woman. Thank you
that I'm not like that nasty little tax
man over there ..."
'Taxman sneaks into the Temple.
Heads turn. "What's he doing here?"
He's out of place – and he knows it.
He's as welcome as a skinhead in a
five-star hotel.
**'But he wants to pray. He must
pray.**
'He finds a dark corner at the back.

He stands staring at the floor. He
strikes his fists against his chest again
and again.
' "Oh God, I'm sorry. Oh God, I'm
ashamed. Oh God, I'm the worst man
on earth! Have pity!"

**'Pharisee strides out of the Temple.
He'll be back shortly for another talk
with himself.**
**'Taxman sneaks out of the Temple.
He may never come back. But God
goes with him.'**

7
PEACE MISSION

Peace is what happens
when heaven and earth overlap.

Peace of body

5·12-16

Once Jesus was in a town where there was a man who was suffering from a dreaded skin-disease ...

Jesus is surprised. People are shrieking and running in all directions. A minute ago there was a crowded street. Now the whole place is deserted!

And then he sees the reason. **A leper!**

The man falls on the ground in front of Jesus.

'Sir, if you want to, you can make me clean!'

Jesus looks at him. His hair is matted. His clothes are rags – torn rags. Jesus looks again. His flesh is being eaten alive. He's covered in red and white sores. One hand hides his nose and mouth. But that hand is a knotty stump ...

Jesus says nothing. But he does everything. He reaches out and touches the man! A touch that says more than a thousand words. And then he speaks:

'Be clean!'

The golden rule with skin-disease is 'Don't Touch!' Lepers are avoided like the plague. They **are** the plague! But Jesus doesn't shriek and run. He comes and touches.

And instead of him catching the leper's disease, the leper catches his wholeness.

Peace of mind

8·26-39

As Jesus stepped ashore, he was met by a man from the town who had demons in him. For a long time this man had gone without clothes, and would not stay at home ...

His mind is a constant din. His body, a civil war. He has so many evil spirits that they call him 'Mob'!

He wears no clothes, fears no foe, feels no pain. When he's not rampaging round the desert, he's prowling round the tombs. His life is a mini-hell.

He bellows at Jesus: **'Jesus, Son of the Most High God! I beg you, don't punish me!'**

Jewish rulers may not recognize Jesus, but Gentile demons know him well enough. Jesus speaks to them: 'Come out of him – all of you! You can go into those pigs ...'

The demons go into the near-by herd which immediately stampedes into the sea.

Cruelty to animals? A man's life is worth more to God than many sparrows – or pigs!

It's all too much for the locals. **'Mob' cured? The pigs drowned?** They beg Jesus to go away! Somehow he threatens their peace of mind.

Peace of heart

5·17-26

Some men came carrying a paralysed man on a bed, and they tried to take him into the house and put him in front of Jesus. Because of the crowd, however, they could find no way to take him in. So they carried him up on the roof, made an opening in the tiles, and let him down on his bed into the middle of the group in front of Jesus. When Jesus saw how much faith they had, he said to the man, 'Your sins are forgiven, my friend.'

Jesus is teaching. The house is packed. Critics have come from far and wide to see for themselves ...

Suddenly, there's a scrabbling on the roof and a hole appears in the ceiling! Then a bed is lowered into the room and comes to rest at Jesus's feet.

It seems like a student stunt until they see the figure on the bed. **There he lies. An ugly, dejected man. Totally paralysed.**

The critics exchange knowing looks. All that talk of the kingdom of God. This'll bring Jesus down to earth. **This is what life is really like!**

But Jesus isn't thrown by reality. He sees life more clearly than anyone. He says to the man on the bed:

'Your sins are forgiven, my friend.'

There's a gasp of amazement. Jesus has outraged them all. 'Who does he think he is? Only God can forgive sins! He should stick to healing bodies!'

Jesus turns to them: 'I know what you're thinking. But which is easier – to heal a man's legs or forgive a man's life?' They know the answer. To forgive sins is quite impossible unless you have God's authority.

Jesus goes on: 'So to show you that I have God's authority ...' He turns to the paralysed man:

'Get up, pick up your bed, and go home!'

God takes our sin seriously. Sin ruins our life and wrecks our world. There are three ways our sin can be dealt with:

● We can pay for it
● We can be punished for it
● We can be forgiven

Our trouble is that we can never pay the price and never bear the punishment! **Our only hope is forgiveness, and only God can forgive.**

Jesus deals with our real need. Not our paralysed bodies but our guilt-ridden hearts. He comes to offer us forgiveness, God's own cure for heart trouble.

Peace of purpose

9·10-17

When the sun was beginning to set, the twelve disciples came to him and said, 'Send the people away so that they can go to the villages and farms round here and find food and lodging, because this is a lonely place.'

But Jesus said to them, 'You yourselves give them something to eat.'

They answered, 'All we have are five loaves and two fish. Do you want us to go and buy food for this whole crowd?'

John the Baptist is dead. All eyes are on Jesus.

Five thousand men gather to him at Bethsaida. Five thousand men in search of a leader. They hang on his every word. They will follow him anywhere.

Jesus welcomes them. He teaches them all day and at sunset they are still there...

Suddenly the situation is urgent. Five thousand men: tired, hungry, far from home, and excited!

If the cry 'Messiah!' goes up, sticks and swords and clubs and knives will appear from nowhere! The picnic will become a bloodbath...

If the cry 'Messiah!' doesn't go up they will boil over in anger and frustration, robbing villages and raiding farms...

Jesus acts. He takes the only food they have. Five loaves and two fishes. He thanks the Father. He breaks the bread. He shares it round. And as the disciples pass the food they find there's more than enough. **In fact, there's plenty!**

Jesus surveys the scene: five thousand men in the middle of nowhere, having the meal of a lifetime!

And then he sends them home.

Five thousand men offer support. And Jesus turns them down! He is indeed the Messiah, feasting his people with plenty. He is indeed the new Moses, giving bread from heaven for all.

But he has faced this temptation before. His kingdom is not of this world. And he has come to do more than fill stomachs.

Peace on earth

8·22-25

One day Jesus got into a boat with his disciples and said to them, 'Let us go across to the other side of the lake.' So they started out...

Jesus is exhausted. Teaching and healing have taken their toll. He lies on the cushions in the stern and quickly falls asleep.

Meanwhile Peter scans the sky. He doesn't like the look of it. The wind is picking up. The water is dark and restless...

Suddenly a squall hits them! The boat heels alarmingly ...

And then the storm breaks in earnest. Cold winds rip down from the hills, channelled and funnelled by deep ravines. They whip the water into a frenzy ...

In the boat, chaos reigns. The canvas is out of control. The helm won't answer. Timber and tackle groan and whine ...

The disciples are wide-eyed with fear. Not least the fishers among them. Too many friends have been lost this way.

And Jesus? **He's still sound asleep.** There's nothing for it – they'll have to wake him. Any wave now, they'll have to swim for their lives.

'Master, Master! We are about to die!'

Jesus opens his eyes. He takes in the situation: the heaving boat, the panicking men ...

He sits up and speaks sharply **to the weather!**

'Peace! Be still!'

The storm dies instantly! The wind holds its breath. The waves settle and lie down. Galilee is like glass ... They get out the oars.

Jesus looks at the shaken disciples. He's more worried about them!

'Where is your faith?'

Jews are afraid of the sea. And for good reason! So unpredictable, so uncontrollable ... Ever since Noah's Flood they have thanked God for dry land!

To their knowledge only one voice has ever tamed the great deep. The voice of God at creation ... As they lean on the oars, a question forms in each disciple's mind:

'Who is that man in the stern?'

8
OUTSIDE IN

Jesus comes to seek and to save the **lost**. He comes exactly where they are.

Not where they want to be, not where they should be, but where they **are**.

And he always gets the name right.

Embarrassing moment

7.36-50

A Pharisee invited Jesus to have dinner with him, and Jesus went to his house and sat down to eat. In that town was a woman who lived a sinful life. She heard that Jesus was eating in the Pharisee's house ...

Simon the Pharisee is enjoying his meal. A small dinner-party. A few friends. Soft lights. Sweet music. Good food. How kind of Jesus to come. How good of Simon to invite him!

Suddenly there's a disturbance. A servant is trying to stop someone coming in. It's a woman. **Oh no! Not her!**

Some of the guests look embarrassed. They know this woman. Simon blushes. What will Jesus think of him?

The woman is clutching a bottle of perfume. She makes her way round the couches. When she gets to Jesus, she stops. And bursts into tears. She looks a wreck.

Her tears fall hot and wet on Jesus' feet. He lets them. She quickly kneels, unties her hair, wipes the tears away. He lets her.

She gently kisses his feet. He doesn't wince or shrink. Then she takes the stopper from the bottle and pours the perfume all over his feet. And he lets her.

The musty, sexy smell pervades the room. Simon's brain is working overtime. Jesus can't be much of a prophet if he doesn't realize what's going on.

'Simon, I know what you're thinking. But tell me this. Two men are each forgiven a debt. One owes ten times more than the other. Which will be most grateful?'

'Why that's easy. The one who owed the most and was forgiven the most.'

'Quite right! Now compare yourself with this poor woman. You gave me no water when I arrived. She washes my feet with her tears. You gave me no towel. She dries my feet with her hair. You gave me no kiss. She smothers my feet with kisses. You gave me no oil – which is very cheap. But she gives me perfume – which is very expensive!'

Gently, Jesus turns to the woman:

'Your sins are forgiven ... your faith has saved you; go in peace!'

Jesus wants us to come as we are. Hair, perfume, tears and kisses. He loves both the Pharisee and the prostitute. He longs to forgive them both. But while the prostitute admits her need, the Pharisee clings to his pride.

Jesus came for those who know they are lost. Those with tangled emotions. Those with wasted lives. Those who love him.

To them he gives his forgiveness, his healing and his peace.

New life for three

8·40-42, 49-56

When Jesus returned to the other side of the lake, the people welcomed him, because they had all been waiting for him. Then a man named Jairus arrived; he was an official in the local synagogue. He threw himself down at Jesus' feet and begged him to go to his home, because his only daughter, who was twelve years old, was dying.

Everyone wants to see Jesus, but they make way for Jairus. Jairus is an important man. He runs the local synagogue, organizes the services, chooses the preachers! Jesus will bow to Jairus . . .

But what's this? Jairus is flat on his face, begging a favour! 'Jesus! Come to my house for heaven's sake! My daughter is dying – and she's only twelve!'

Jesus agrees. Jairus breathes a sigh of relief. But there's more agony yet! Jesus gets delayed by an old crone. Precious minutes are lost.

And then it's too late. A message arrives for Jairus: 'No need to trouble Jesus after all. She's dead!'

Jairus is an important man. He runs the local synagogue, organizes the services, chooses the preachers . . . But here's a situation that's out of his control. The death of a daughter. His only child . . .

Jesus overhears:

'Don't be afraid; only believe, and she will be well.'

Back at the house, events have moved fast. Professional mourners are already in action. Women are wailing a funeral lament.

Jesus arrives. He doesn't stand on ceremony: **Don't cry. She's only asleep!'**

He clears the house of comforters and shuts the door on everyone except Peter, James and John – and Jairus and his wife.

Outside, the lament turns to mocking laughter. Undertakers known death when they see it. Jesus will have to back down.

Jesus kneels by the girl's bed. He takes her hand. He calls to her:

'Get up, my child!'

Her eyes open. She smiles.

Jairus's daughter is restored to life. And not only his daughter! Jairus and his wife are alive again too!

A hand in the crowd

8·42-48

As Jesus went along, the people were crowding him from every side. Among them was a woman who had suffered from severe bleeding for twelve years ... She came up in the crowd behind Jesus and touched the edge of his cloak ...

Galilee welcomes Jesus! They are glad to have him back. He's been across the lake too long. They cheer. They shout. They chant slogans. They push and pat and pinch and press. **And in that crowd is a woman who just has to get to Jesus!**

Poor woman. For twelve long years she has been bleeding. For twelve long years she has been 'unclean'. Anything she touches must be washed. That's the Law. Anyone who touches her must bathe. That's the Law. She can't go to the synagogue. She can't go to the shops. She can't go anywhere. That's the Law.

Her illness has puzzled the doctors, disgusted her husband, embarrassed her friends. This is her last chance. She must get a hand to Jesus. And she makes it! As her fingers touch his cloak, a wonderful peace flows through her and her bleeding stops. Thankfully she slips away.

But Jesus calls out: 'Someone touched me. Who was it?'

Peter can't believe his ears. What does Jesus mean? Is there anyone in the crowd who **hasn't** touched him?

But Jesus insists. 'Someone touched me. I felt power go out of me.'

There is silence. Jesus waits. Then the woman comes to the front. She falls at Jesus' feet. She is thin and pale and trembling.

'Master – it was I who touched you. I touched the edge of your cloak. And, Master – I'm better!'

Jesus is glad she's come into the open. 'My daughter, there's nothing magic about my cloak. It's your faith that has made you well!'

Jesus is glad she's come into the open. Now she won't feel she has stolen from him. Now all will know that she's been healed. Now they'll expect to see her around. Now they'll welcome her at church.

Jesus is glad she's come into the open. Healing is free, but it isn't cheap. Her healing costs Jesus a lot. He feels drained of power.

Do we think sin costs nothing? God will hardly notice it? If so, we're wrong! Our sin costs God his Son. Our sin costs Jesus his life.

Jesus is glad she's come into the open.

'My daughter, your faith has made you well. Go in peace.'

She came to Jesus empty-handed. She leaves with a heart full of peace. The beautiful, lasting peace of Christ.

Bent double

13·10-17

One Sabbath Jesus was teaching in a synagogue. A woman there had an evil spirit in her that had made her ill for eighteen years; she was bent over and could not straighten up at all.

Bent double. She's been like it for as long as anyone can remember.

She shuffles into church. She says 'good morning' to the row of feet at the door. Makes her way to her usual seat. Puts her walking stick beside her. Stares miserably at her kneeler.

How hard life is!

Slowly a voice begins to break into her thoughts; the warm, understanding voice of a young teacher. He's calling her! Has she fallen asleep? She's so used to her mind wandering during the service. After all, no-one talks to the women in a synagogue.

Suddenly she feels a surge of hope. It's years since anyone has taken any notice of her.

All this time she's been turned in on herself, not just by a bent back, but by an inward-looking mind. Even in church she's been hunched up, thinking only of herself, her regrets, her miseries.

But Jesus puts a stop to that. He touches her. He speaks to her.

'Woman, you are free!'

Free! Free to stand up straight. Free to look the world in the eye. Free to notice the needs of others. Free to look God in the face and praise him!

But the leader of the synagogue protests! 'Jesus is breaking the Law! He's working on the Sabbath. Not even doctors are allowed to work today unless it's to save a life.'

But Jesus answers: 'You frauds! You work on the Sabbath too. You untie your animals and give them water. So why can't I untie this woman?

'The Sabbath is God's day. And God wants his children to be free. So what better day to untie them?'

Listener's lib

10·38-42

As Jesus and his disciples went on their way, he came to a village where a woman named Martha welcomed him

in her home. She had a sister named Mary ...

Martha and Mary are sisters. Martha – active and out-going. Mary – quiet and thoughtful.

You still see them today: Martha running for President, Mary walking to the library.

Martha welcomes the men with food! She conjures dish after dish from the kitchen.

Mary helps as best she can: waiting at table, washing the bowls. As she works, she listens.

Mary has never been to school, never written a letter, never read a book. Jesus is the first teacher she has ever understood. She pauses near him. She stands there for some time. Somehow the food doesn't seem so important. She's bursting to ask questions, and dying to laugh!

At last she sits at the master's feet and forgets the cooking altogether.

Suddenly there's an explosion! Martha erupts from the kitchen. She towers over Jesus.

'Lord, don't you care that my sister has left me to do all the work by myself? Tell her to come and help me!'

Jesus knows how Martha feels. But he also understands Mary.

'Martha! Martha! You are worried and troubled over so many things – One course after another! But only one thing is really needed – and that's the word of God. Mary has chosen to listen. It's not for me or anyone else to stop her.'

Jesus says one thing is needed. Not health or wealth or long life. Not wit or wisdom or good friends. Just one thing – and that's to listen to God.

Zacchaeus

19·1-10

Jesus went on into Jericho and was passing through. There was a chief tax collector there named Zacchaeus, who was rich ...

Zacchaeus is a little man. Stunted – in many ways. But in the world of commerce, Zacchaeus is big. Chief Inspector of Taxes!

But his success has cost him dear. A tax collector can't be rich **and** popular! He collects money for the Romans and he keeps plenty for himself. Small wonder that he has no friends.

Zacchaeus hears that Jesus is coming: Jesus – the friend of sinners!

Jesus – the friend of tax collectors!

Zacchaeus must see Jesus. But he's so small. The crowd won't let him to the front. Not even if he faints.

So he goes ahead of the crowd. He climbs a tree, a sycamore tree, a big tree with low branches, an easy tree to climb.

Zacchaeus waits. The crowd gathers. The noise gets louder. He peers through the leaves to catch a glimpse ...

And what a surprise! He sees a warm smile and laughing eyes. He hears a friendly voice!

'Zacchaeus – hurry up and come down! I must stay at your home today!'

Is this a joke? No-one has smiled at

him for years! No-one has been to his house since he moved in! Are they going to make fun of him? Tease him for trying to see? Jostle and bundle and poke him all the way home?

Zacchaeus has no doubts. He makes haste. He comes down. He receives Jesus – joyfully!

Many people in the town of Jericho would gladly have had Jesus to stay. Many God-fearing, respectable people: priests and teachers, doctors and lawyers, housewives and secretaries.

But Jesus decides for himself. And he chooses Zacchaeus. Time-serving, double-dealing, money-grabbing Zacchaeus! The name that makes all Jericho spit. The name they never speak in love. The house they never enter willingly.

Jericho is the lowest town in the world, Seven hundred feet below sea-level. Zacchaeus is the lowest man in the lowest town. And that's where Jesus comes! Why does Jesus stoop so low? Why does he let the side down, pick bad company, mingle with the dregs?

Because Jesus comes to seek and to save the lost! And he comes exactly where they are. Not where they want to be, not where they should be, but where they are.

He knows the hiding place at a desk, on a roof, by a well. Even up a tree! He knows, he comes, he calls. And he always gets the name right!

Beggars can be choosers

18.35-43

As Jesus was coming near Jericho, there was a blind man sitting by the road, begging ...

Jesus comes to Jericho. The tension mounts. From here it's only seventeen miles to Jerusalem.

History is being made. The Son of David is coming to the City of David. Neither will ever be the same again.

The crowd sweeps in through the city gate. No-one thinks twice about the beggars. Suddenly one of them starts to shout. He shouts at the top of his voice something no-one else even dares to whisper!

'Jesus, Son of David! Jesus, Son of David!'

Jesus has never been called Messiah in public before. The beggar can see, with both eyes shut, that Jesus is the Son of God.

Desperately, people try to shut him up. This is no time for beggars. This is no time for underground slogans. It could start a riot. It could lead to bloodshed.

'Shut up!'

But the beggar won't shut up. He shouts and shouts until his voice is a high-pitched scream:

'Son of David! Take pity on me!'

He is straining and shrieking like a mad dog on a chain ... And Jesus stops. He comes over to the beggar.

'What do you want me to do for you?'

What a question to ask a blind man! The beggar can choose whatever he wants. He can ask for money, or food, or clothes, or friendship. But he knows what he wants and he comes right out with it.

'Sir, I want to see again.'

Jesus says:

'Then see! Your faith has made you well.'

It was the last miracle before Jesus' arrest. And the most complete. The man was a beggar. And he was blind. When Jesus healed him, he used his sight to follow the master. And everyone who saw it praised God.

From now on beggars **can** be choosers! The Messiah has come.

9
SEE-THROUGH
SAYINGS

Jesus is a prophet.
He has God's eye-view of the world.
He sees through the present.
He sees through the future.

Bad acting

11·37 – 12·3

As thousands of people crowded together, so that they were stepping on each other, Jesus said first to his disciples, 'Be on guard against the yeast of the Pharisees – I mean their hypocrisy.'

Pharisees have it all worked out! They are experts on how to be holy. And it's all done by keeping the rules. Rules for every occasion. Washing and eating, sleeping and greeting, working or resting. You name it, it's on the list!

If cleanliness is next to godliness, then Pharisees are God's bodyguard! But Jesus sees through them. It's all an act. And a bad act at that.

'You clean the outside, rinse your fingers, wash the plates. **But what about the inside?** You fuss and fiddle, counting strides, weighing loads, tithing tea-leaves. **But what about justice? What about love?**

'You like the front seats in the synagogue; you like the low bows in the market. **But it's all an act!**

'People hope to catch your holiness. Little do they know they are catching corruption.'

Then Jesus rounds on the lawyers: the men who make the rules and then expect applause for keeping them.

'You lawyers, you're just as bad. You load on laws until no-one can possibly keep them all. But you leave nice little loop-holes for yourselves.

'You and your fathers make a good team: they kill the prophets; you build the tombs!

'Why is it that you always miss the point? You know the way to God but you never go to him. **And you prevent others from knowing.**'

Jesus saw many wretched sights: hunger, disease, poverty, injustice . . .

But to him the worst of them all was hypocrisy. Bad acting.

A cry from the heart

19·41-44

He came closer to the city, and when he saw it he wept over it, saying, 'If you only knew today what is needed for peace! But now you cannot see it! The time will come when your enemies will surround you with barricades, blockade you, and close in on you from every side. They will completely destroy you and the people within your walls; not a single stone will they leave in its place, because you did not recognize the time when God came to save you!'

They round the final bend. They come within sight of the city. The joyful shouts of the pilgrim army become a deafening roar. And Jesus bursts into tears. He weeps with uncontrollable sobs.

Stretched out before him lies Jerusalem, the city of God. Jesus sees what is. And he sees what might have been.

The Jews have often prayed for the peace of Jerusalem. But they have never made their own peace with God. And without God there is no peace.

The Messiah has come to make peace. But they can't see him as he really is. They see him only through dark glasses of pride and hatred. They see only what they want to see. An army. An uprising. The chance to put Jerusalem on the map.

But Jesus sees the truth. In a few short years, Roman armies will surround the city. They will lay siege to her. They will break her. **They will wipe her off the map.**

Why? Because God will judge his city. The city that has missed God's moment. The city that has killed God's Son.

We can reject God as our Saviour. But he will still come as our Judge.

No time for the Temple

21.5-7

Some of the disciples were talking about the Temple, how beautiful it looked with its fine stones and the gifts offered to God.

The newest Temple was built by Herod the Great, for his glory. At least it was started by Herod, and took nearly fifty years to complete.

In fact it was finished just in time for the Roman Emperor to burn it down!

Tourists never tire of the Temple. And the disciples are no exception. They admire the rows of columns, each one forty feet high, each one made of solid marble.

They admire the mighty vine. A giant family tree. Symbol of Israel. Solid gold! With man-sized bunches of grapes!

They shield their eyes from the glory, the glaring white, the blazing gold.

What a fabulous Temple! What a fitting place for God!

Suddenly Jesus brings them down to earth.

'The time will come, and it won't be long, when everything you see – the courtyards, the colonnades, the sanctuary – everything will be demolished. Not a stone will be left standing!'

The disciples are staggered. Twelve sets of lips frame a single question: 'Teacher, when will this be? How will we know when it's about to happen?'

So Jesus tells them of two crises:

● The short-term crisis: the end of Jerusalem.
● The long-term crisis: the end of the age.

The two crises will take place at different times. But they will both be the work of God.

Two crises

21·20-28

● **Short-term crisis:**
The end of Jerusalem.
'When you see Jerusalem surrounded by armies, then you will know that she will soon be destroyed.'

Jesus repeatedly warns of a violent end for Jerusalem. God will finally judge his people. They have abused his love. They have killed his messengers. They have rejected his Son. God will give them what they so richly deserve.

Jesus has urgent advice: 'When the judgement comes, run to the hills! Don't think you'll be safe in the city. Don't think God will spare Jerusalem. He won't!

'Woe betide the expectant mothers and the babes in arms and the toddlers. They won't stand a chance!'

It will be a terrible day. The Day of the Lord!

And so it was. Forty years later, in AD 70, Jerusalem was surrounded by the armies of Titus. Thousands of Jews were killed or captured. It was the blackest day in their long history.

The population was butchered. The Temple was burned.

By the time the soldiers and looters had finished their rampage, it was possible to pull a plough across the site, from one side of the city to the other.

● **Long-term crisis:**
The end of the Age.
'There will be strange things happening to the sun, the moon, and the stars. On earth, whole countries will be in despair, afraid of the roar of the sea and the raging tides.'

God's judgement of Jerusalem is just a foretaste of his judgement on the world. History is going somewhere. It's not just a weary tread-mill of life and death. It's not just a dreary cycle of seasons.

History has a meaning, and the meaning is Christ.

As history moves towards its climax there will be cosmic upheaval and world chaos. There will be terror in the natural elements and despair in the human heart.

But the bad news will give way to good news! When all seems lost, Jesus Christ will appear in his kingly power. He will come to judge the world and save his people.

When will this be? Nobody knows. We must read the signs of the times. We must live each day in the light of eternity.

First the bad news

21·8-19

'Before all these things take place, however, you will be arrested and persecuted; you will be handed over to be tried in synagogues and be put in prison; you will be brought before kings and rulers for my sake.'

Jesus warns his disciples of three developments:

● **Hard times**
Dark days lie ahead for the followers of Jesus. They will be harassed and hindered, persecuted and provoked. They will be arrested, dragged before the courts, thrown into prison.

The world that hates Jesus will scarcely love his followers! But like the plagues before the escape from Egypt these trials will give birth to God's victory.

● **Fake Messiahs**
There will be many imitation Christs.

'Many men, claiming to speak for me, will come and say, "I am he!" and "The time has come!"'
Don't be fooled, don't be afraid, and don't follow them! No-one knows the time of the end. That's something only God knows.

● **Frequent disasters**
In the last days there will always be bad news:

'There will be terrible earthquakes, famines and plagues everywhere; there will be strange and terrifying things coming from the sky.'
Revolution and war. Famine and plague. Earthquake and eclipse. These events are facts of life, the fatal symptoms of our dying world. We must live with the tension they create until Christ comes again.

Then the good news

21·27-28,34-36

'When these things begin to happen, stand up and raise your heads, because your salvation is near.'

When are the last days? They are now! They stretch from the day Jesus was raised from the dead until the day he comes again in glory.

To all who worry, Jesus says: 'Don't panic! I will come again!
'Never give way to despair. Don't drown your sorrows or gnaw your nails. When others lose their heads, make sure you keep yours!
'Every headline is a signpost and it points to me. I am the end!'

10
RISING RAGE

Jesus is a peasant from Galilee,
a carpenter by trade,
a preacher by calling.

They don't like his face,
they don't like his voice,
and they don't want his news.

Lord of the flies!

11·14-23

Jesus was driving out a demon that could not talk; and when the demon went out, the man began to talk. The crowds were amazed, but some of the people said, 'It is Beelzebul, the chief of the demons, who gives him the power to drive them out.'

Jesus has power over demons. His enemies can't deny it. But they have their own explanation.

'Of course, you know how he gets the power? It comes from Beelzebul, The Lord of the Flies! He has power over demons because he's in league with them.'

But Jesus answers them: 'If I destroy evil with evil there's civil war in hell. Satan must be losing his grip. His troops are fighting each other!

'But tell me. How do **your** men throw out demons? Who are **they** in league with?'

It's a good question. And there's only one answer.

Satan's house is being burgled. The blind are seeing. The deaf are hearing. The lame are walking. The dumb are speaking.

There's only one burglar who leaves finger-prints like that. His name is God.

Who says?

20·1-8

One day, when Jesus was in the Temple teaching the people and preaching the Good News, the chief priests and the teachers of the Law, together with the elders, came and said to him, 'Tell us, what right do you have to do these things? Who gave you this right?' Jesus answered them, 'Now let me ask you a question ...'

Jesus is a peasant from Galilee, a carpenter by trade, a preacher by calling ...

The religious leaders don't like his face, don't like his voice, don't want his good news. But they can't ignore him any longer.

He has entered the city, he has cleared the Temple, he is teaching huge crowds.

They decide the best form of defence is attack! 'Tell us ... what right do you have to do these things? Where are your qualifications? Who were your teachers?'

Jesus can't win. If he says, 'God gave me the right,' he'll be arrested for blasphemy. If he says, 'No-one gave me the right,' he'll quickly lose support.

But two can play at this game! Jesus answers the question with a question:

'You tell me: did John's right to baptize come from God?'

Now **they** can't win. If they say, 'Yes,' they'll be admitting they were wrong to ignore John. If they say, 'No,' they'll be shouted down and even stoned by the crowd.

Just think. If they had answered Jesus's question correctly, they'd have also found the answer to their own!

Trick question

20·19-26

'Tell us, is it against our Law for us to pay taxes to the Roman Emperor, or not?' But Jesus saw through their trick and said to them, 'Show me a silver coin ...'

It's a burning issue. Every man and woman in the Empire has to pay a coin a year to the Emperor. And of course the Jews hate it! They strongly believe that they should only pay tax to God.

It's a burning issue. But it's also a trick. The men who ask the question are spies, sent by religious leaders to catch Jesus out.

'Is it against our Law to pay taxes to the Roman Emperor, or not?'

Jesus can't win. If he says, 'Yes, it's God's will that you pay taxes to Rome,' he'll outrage the Jews. If he says, 'No, it's God's will that you stop paying tax,' he'll be arrested for civil disobedience.

Jesus doesn't answer straight away. He asks if anyone has a Roman coin. A really strict Jew wouldn't dirty his pocket with such a coin, but someone has one! Jesus looks at the image of Tiberius Caesar on the silver. He asks them a question:

'Whose face and name are these on it?'

'Why, the Emperor's, of course!'

And then Jesus gives them their answer:

'This coin bears Caesar's image. Caesar gives you good order, good protection and good roads. These things have to be paid for!

'But forget about this coin. What about **yourselves**? Whose image do **you** bear?'

You are made in the image of God. God gives you life and health and joy and peace.

'So give Caesar his taxes. But give yourselves to God.'

Silly riddle

20·27-40

Then some Sadducees, who say that people will not rise from death, came to Jesus ...

Sadducees are born to rule. They control the Temple. They control the treasury. And they want to keep it that way! So they don't annoy the Romans, and they steer clear of God.

Sadducees don't believe in the supernatural. They don't believe in life after death. It's impossible.

They put their point to Jesus: 'Moses said a man must marry his brother's widow to continue the family line. But what happens if a woman marries one brother after another? What happens if she marries **seven** brothers? Who's wife will she be in heaven?

'You see? Eternal life is impossible!'

It's a silly question. They aren't really serious. But Jesus gives them a serious answer:

'You don't know what you're talking about! You assume God is no more powerful than you. Don't you see? Heaven is a different sort of life. There'll be no marriage for a start.'

He goes on: 'You know, there **is** life after death. And Scripture tells you so. God introduced himself to Moses as "the God of Abraham, Isaac and Jacob". Those men are with God **now**. Real life is friendship with God. And that doesn't stop with death.

'Death doesn't take God's friends from him. It takes them to him!'

11
THE
WAY OUT

For Jesus there is no way out.
His road leads to Jerusalem.
His ladder to heaven is a wooden cross.

But God's way out is man's way in.

Royal event

19·28-40

As he came near Bethphage and Bethany at the Mount of Olives, he sent two disciples ahead with these instructions: 'Go to the village there ahead of you; as you go in, you will find a colt tied up that has never been ridden. Untie it and bring it here. If someone asks you why you are untying it, tell him that the Master needs it.'

They went on their way and found everything just as Jesus had told them. As they were untying the colt, its owners said to them, 'Why are you untying it?'

'The Master needs it,' they answered, and they took the colt to Jesus. Then they threw their cloaks over the animal and helped Jesus get on. As he rode on, people spread their cloaks on the road.

When he came near Jerusalem, at the place where the road went down the Mount of Olives, the large crowd of his disciples began to thank God and praise him in loud voices for all the great things that they had seen: 'God bless the king who comes in the name of the Lord! Peace in heaven and glory to God!'

Jesus rides from the Mount of Olives, at the head of a pilgrim army. And yet he comes humbly – riding a borrowed ass!

He is Prince of Peace.

The crowds take up the theme:

'God bless the king who comes in the name of the Lord! Peace in heaven, and glory to God.'

The peace of heaven is being poured out on earth. Echoes of angels!

As Jesus rides on, they carpet the road with clothes. They want him to ride over their lives, and take his royal throne.

Like David before him, Jesus will never proclaim himself king. He will only be king when everyone welcomes him.

He certainly gets no welcome from the Pharisees: 'Teacher, command your disciples to be quiet!' They don't want troops moving in to break up the festival. And anyway, they don't believe Jesus is the Messiah.

But Jesus tells them this is no time for silence:

'I tell you that if they keep quiet, the stones themselves will start shouting.'

The whole of history has been moving to this time and place. The walls of Jerusalem have been waiting for this moment, ever since they were built.

If men won't greet God's Messiah, then the bricks in the wall and the boulders by the road will burst into songs of praise!

Clean-up campaign

19·45-48

Jesus went into the Temple and began to drive out the merchants ...

Jesus comes to the Temple. A place he loves.

He came as a baby to be blessed. He came as a teenager to ask questions. He came as an adult to worship. Now he comes as Messiah to take charge.

He enters the Court of the Gentiles, the only place in the Temple where outsiders can come and pray. He stands and looks and listens.

The courtyard is a hive of activity. Money-changers are standing at little desks: 'Get your temple coins here! Market traders are shouting their wares: 'Salt and flour, oil and wine! Get your incense here!'

Priests are herding goats and rams, calves and oxen. Some are selling doves and pigeons. 'Sacrifices! Get your birds and animals here! Temple-inspected sacrifices ...'

Jesus has seen the sight many times. Today he can stand it no longer. This is his Father's house, not a supermarket, not a cattle ranch, not a short-cut or a bank.

This is his Father's house, a place where anyone can come and be still and know God. And yet poor pilgrims are being hassled, exploited, fleeced and robbed.

Jesus waits no longer. In a one-man demo he throws them all out!

'It is written in the Scriptures that God said, "My Temple will be called a house of prayer." But you have turned it into a hideout for thieves!'

So Jesus clears the Temple. In so doing he seals his own fate.

But for the time being he is safe. He stays in the Temple and teaches. Anyone trying to arrest him will get rough treatment from the fans!

Satan makes a move

22·1-6

The time was near for the Festival of Unleavened Bread, which is called the Passover. The chief priests and the teachers of the Law were afraid of the people, and so they were trying to find a way of putting Jesus to death secretly. Then Satan entered Judas, called Iscariot, who was one of the twelve disciples.

'Jesus' is the name on everyone's lips. The crowded festival streets are buzzing with speculation: will he stand for Messiah? Throw out the Romans? Sort out the Jews?

The average pilgrim hopes he will. The average priest hopes he won't. But the leaders aren't leaving anything to chance.

Now Satan makes a move. Since the baptism of Jesus, he has lost every round. His cover has been blown and his city besieged. Now he penetrates the inner circle. He enters Judas.

Why Judas? We may never know. He had always been charming, alert, and reliable. They had even trusted him with their money! Did he need the money? Did he want to speed up events? Did he resent the talk of suffering and death?

We know little of Judas, but Satan hasn't changed. He still tries the same old temptation: 'Help yourself!'

Maximum security

22.7-13

The day came during the Festival of Unleavened Bread when the lambs for the Passover meal were to be killed. Jesus sent off Peter and John with these instructions: 'Go and get the Passover meal ready for us to eat.' 'Where do you want us to get it ready?' they asked him. He answered, 'As you go into the city, a man carrying a jar of water will meet you. Follow him ...'

The net is closing. But Jesus is in control. He plays it very close: no name, no address, and a secret sign.

A man carrying water will lead them to the house with an Upper Room. There won't be more than one man carrying water, because it's women's work! Jesus chooses his most trusted pair, Peter and John, to prepare the room and the meal.

Passover looks back to the rescue of the Hebrew slaves from Egypt. It looks forward to the heavenly banquet in the kingdom of God. The menu is always the same:

● **Roast Lamb** On their last night in Egypt, each Hebrew household killed a lamb. They ate the meat, and daubed the blood over the outside door. When the angel of death saw the blood of the lamb, he 'passed over' the house and spared the life of their eldest son.

● **Unleavened bread** All yeast is cleared from the house, as a sign that evil is thrown out. Then bread is made without yeast, to recall the escape from Egypt. They left in such a hurry that there was no time to let the dough rise!

● **Bitter herbs** To remind everyone of the bitterness of the slavery in Egypt.

● **Mixed fruit** Apples, dates, figs and raisins, all mixed together to look like mud! The Hebrew slaves had to make bricks out of mud for the Egyptians.

● **A flagon of wine** The wine is red, diluted with water. Four cups of wine are passed round during the Passover meal.

A new Passover

22·14-20

When the hour came, Jesus took his place at the table with the apostles. He said to them, 'I have wanted so much to eat this Passover meal with you before I suffer!'

Jesus has given much thought to this meal. It will be the last they will have before all hell breaks loose. The coming events will take Jesus to the cross and drive the disciples into hiding. How can he sum up all he has been, all he has done, all he is and will do?

He pours the wine. He gives thanks to God. He passes the cup.
'Take this and share it among yourselves.'

For Jesus there is to be no more wine-tasting until they all meet again at the Messiah's banquet in the kingdom of God.

He takes the bread. He gives thanks to God. He breaks it. He passes it round.

'This is my body which is given for you. Do this in memory of me.'

The bread is a visual aid. Just as the bread is broken and shared, so his body will be broken for all.

After the meal there is another toast. Jesus passes the cup:
'This cup is God's new covenant sealed with my blood, which is poured out for you.'

The wine is a visual aid. Just as it is poured out and passed round, so his blood will be shed for all. It will set the seal on God's new promise.

For the disciples, the Passover meal will never be the same again. Jesus has given it new meaning. The bread is now his broken body. The wine is now his poured-out life.

A New Exodus is about to take place. God is making a new way out for his people. He is providing an escape from sin and death. And God is providing a perfect Passover lamb.

The lamb is his Son Jesus Christ. Through his blood a New Israel will be born: the Christian church.

On the rack

22·39-46

Jesus left the city and went, as he usually did, to the Mount of Olives; and the disciples went with him. When he arrived at the place, he said to them, 'Pray that you will not fall into
temptation.' Then he went off from them about the distance of a stone's throw and knelt down and prayed.

Their last supper is over. A deep horror creeps over Jesus. There is nothing between himself and the end.

He prays.

Every victory of his life has been

won in prayer. The battle to reject Satan; the battle to understand his calling; the battle to free sick bodies and dark minds; the battle to choose and train disciples.

Now he fights the most important battle of all. The battle for the right state of mind. The battle to fight desertion by friends, rejection by foes, and death by torture. The battle to bear the sin of the whole world.

'Father, are you sure there is no other way? Must I really drink this poison? Must it really be this year?

'Look at my disciples! They still haven't a clue. They still squabble among themselves. They still hope for an uprising.

'Look at Peter! Fast asleep – clutching a sword! He swears he'll stick with me, but he won't. Even his big heart will break tonight.'

And then all the old temptations return – a thousand times worse! 'Take the easy way.' 'Settle for world power.' 'You've made your point. Spare us the finale . . .'

Jesus is on the rack. The cross starts here. Hanging between earth and heaven, torn between love and fear, pierced to the heart.

Waves of nausea and shock sweep over him. Sweat pours off his face and body. Cold sweat. Like blood.

The entire plan of God is in the balance. If Jesus loses this battle, then all is lost. But Jesus doesn't lose. He prays the prayer he taught others: 'Father – Your will be done. Your will to save mankind. Your will that I die for others. Your will that I take the punishment of the world. **Not my will, but yours!'**

Jesus is exhausted. But he has won a vital victory – the victory to go willingly to the cross.

He goes not as a struggling animal, not even as a stoic martyr. He goes as a loving and obedient Son. And that's the only way to go.

He gets up and goes in search of his disciples. They are fast asleep.

In the net

22·47-53

Jesus was still speaking when a crowd arrived, led by Judas, one of the twelve disciples. He came up to Jesus to kiss him. But Jesus said, 'Judas, is it with a kiss that you betray the Son of Man?'

When the disciples who were with Jesus saw what was going to happen, they asked, 'Shall we use our swords, Lord?' And one of them struck the High Priest's slave and cut off his right ear. But Jesus said, 'Enough of this!' He touched the man's ear and healed him.

The net closes.

Enter Judas, with a small army: leading priests and rulers, Roman soldiers, Temple police with swords, back-street ruffians with clubs. An unholy alliance!

They come through the trees with torches and lanterns. But Jesus makes no move to escape. It's almost too dark to see. The soldiers will arrest whoever Judas kisses. **He kisses Jesus.**

Peter realizes the trap. He takes a wild swipe with his sword, and catches a slave's ear! It would be funny if it weren't so tragic. Jesus tells him to stop.

Even as they move to bind his wrists, he reaches out to heal the jagged ear. He came not to hurt but to heal.

Then Jesus said to the chief priests and the officers of the Temple guard and the elders who had come there to get him, 'Did you have to come with swords and clubs, as though I were an outlaw? I was with you in the Temple every day, and you did not try to arrest me. But this is your hour to act, when the power of darkness rules.'

This is a cowardly, hole-in-the-corner arrest. Jesus asks some pointed questions:

'Why didn't you arrest me in daylight? Why didn't you arrest me in the Temple?' And why are you armed to the teeth? Am I well known for violence?'

No-one looks him in the eye. And there is no reply.

Judas betrays Jesus with a kiss. Peter betrays Jesus with a sword. The rest betray Jesus by slipping away into the darkness . . .

Rough justice

22·54-65

They arrested Jesus and took him away into the house of the High Priest; and Peter followed at a distance. A fire had been lit in the centre of the courtyard, and Peter joined those who were sitting round it. When one of the servant girls saw him sitting there at the fire, she looked straight at him and said, 'This man too was with Jesus!'

But Peter denied it, 'Woman, I don't even know him!'

After a little while, a man noticed Peter and said, 'You are one of them, too!'

But Peter answered, 'Man, I am not!'

And about an hour later another man insisted strongly, 'There isn't any doubt that this man was with Jesus, because he also is a Galilean!'

But Peter answered, 'Man, I don't know what you are talking about!'

At once, while he was still speaking, a cock crowed. The Lord turned round and looked straight at Peter, and Peter remembered that the Lord had said to him, 'Before the cock crows tonight, you will say three times that you do not know me.' Peter went out and wept bitterly.

The men who were guarding Jesus mocked him and beat him. They blindfolded him and asked him, 'Who hit you? Guess!' And they said many other insulting things to him.

Tomorrow is Passover. The High Priest and his friends must work fast. They want Jesus dead – and quick!

Peter slips into the courtyard and finds a place with the servants and bystanders round the fire. From there he can see everything. He can see Jesus being cross-questioned. He can see the rulers with their heads together, planning their next moves.

Suddenly, Peter has problems of his own. The servants notice his northern accent, and recognize him as a disciple of Jesus. Suddenly he's scared for his own safety. Time and again he denies knowing Jesus! In the end he's shouting at the top of his voice.

'He's nothing to do with me!'

Jesus hears his friend. He turns to look across the yard.

A cock crows. Dawn breaks. And Peter's heart breaks too.

When the priests have finished their interrogation, they leave Jesus under guard. The sentries amuse themselves with Blind Man's Buff – for sadists.

Rough justice? Rough – certainly. Justice – never.

Fixing the facts

22·66–23·1

When day came, the elders, the chief priests, and the teachers of the Law met together, and Jesus was brought before the Council. 'Tell us,' they said, 'are you the Messiah?'

He answered, 'If I tell you, you will not believe me; and if I ask you a question, you will not answer. But from now on the Son of Man will be seated on the right of Almighty God.'

They all said, 'Are you, then, the Son of God?'

He answered them, 'You say that I am.'

And they said, 'We don't need any witnesses! We ourselves have heard what he said!'

The whole group rose up and took Jesus before Pilate ...

In the morning, Jesus is brought before the Jewish Council. Their aim is to pin on him a charge of blasphemy. The Council is in a hurry:

● They should begin by hearing the case for the defence. But they have already arrived at their own conclusion.

● They should not be hearing such a serious case on the eve of Passover. But they are.

● They should not try, convict and execute a man all on the same day. But they will.

They ask Jesus: **'Are you the Messiah?'**

Jesus has always avoided the title 'Messiah'. It smacks too much of nationalism and revolt. He prefers the title 'Son of Man' – the one who is to come in glory at the end of the age.

So the Council ask him point blank: **'Are you, then, the Son of God?'**

Jesus answers: 'You could put it like that.'

That's all they need to know. Jesus has claimed to be on a level with Almighty God. He is guilty of blasphemy. The penalty is death.

Without further delay, Jesus is taken to Pontius Pilate, the Roman Governor. The Jewish Council can find him guilty of blasphemy; but only the Roman Governor can have him put to death.

Passing the buck

23·1-25

The whole group rose up and took Jesus before Pilate ...

Pontius Pilate couldn't care less about blasphemy. He doesn't believe in God anyway! The Council know this. So on their way to see Pilate, they switch the charge. They change it from blasphemy to treason.

'This man is a troublemaker. He tells people not to pay taxes. He claims to be king of the Jews!'

Pilate isn't worried. He finds it all rather amusing. **'Are you the king of the Jews?'**

Jesus answers: 'The words are yours.'

Pilate turns to the accusers: 'Let him go! There's always some tin-pot Messiah turning up. I'm sorry he's deluded, but I don't wish him dead.'

Pilate is a hard man to shift. But they know how to move him. 'This man is dangerous! He's come down here from Galilee. Jerusalem is packed with his supporters ...'

Pilate pricks up his ears at the mention of Galilee. 'Galilee? That's Herod's problem. Take him to Herod – he's here for the feast. After all, one king of the Jews should be interested to meet another!'

Herod was very pleased when he saw Jesus ...

Herod Antipas likes party tricks. He wants Jesus to show him some miracles. But Jesus disappoints him. The accused man says nothing. And does nothing.

Herod and his soldiers decide to entertain themselves. They dress Jesus in a royal robe, and give him a mock coronation. When they get tired of laughing, they send him back to Pilate still wearing fancy dress.

Pilate likes the joke so much that Herod and he become firm friends.

Pilate called together the chief priests, the leaders, and the people ...

Pilate tries another loophole. Every Passover he releases a popular prisoner. This year he plans to release Jesus.

But the crowd has different ideas. When they see Jesus, exhausted and beaten, they refuse to have him. They shout for another prisoner – Barabbas. At least Barabbas is a man of action. He has a riot and a murder to his credit already.

Pilate shouts at the crowd: 'All right, I'll have Jesus flogged and set him free!'

But the mob want blood. 'To the cross with him!' 'To the cross!'

So Pilate gives in. He has more important things to do. He gives Barabbas a free pardon and he gives Jesus a death sentence.

As good as dead

23·26-31

The soldiers led Jesus away ...
From the moment he leaves the judgement hall, from the moment he shoulders the wooden beam, **Jesus is as good as dead.**

Four Roman soldiers escort him out of the city. They are heading for 'The Skull', the place of execution, the place outside the city, beyond the pale.

They take the long way round through the blood-thirsty mob.

Jesus is as good as dead. The women start up a funeral lament. They weep and wail for the nice young man. Jesus gathers strength to speak: 'Don't weep for me. Weep for yourselves! If this is what happens to me, think what will happen to you!'

Jesus is as good as dead. The crowd can do whatever they like. They jeer and whistle and hiss. They throw rubbish and rotten fruit.

In the end, Jesus collapses. He sinks under the weight of the cross. His back is raw. His strength is gone. The carpenter of Nazareth can no longer shoulder a plank of wood.

The soldiers volunteer a man in the crowd to carry the cross-piece for him. His name is Simon; an African from modern Tripoli. He will remember this holy day for the rest of his life.

The last laugh?

23·32-43

Two other men, both of them criminals, were also led out to be put to death with Jesus. When they came to the place called 'The Skull' they crucified Jesus there, and the two criminals, one on his right and the other on his left.

The Son of God is stripped, tripped, thrown headlong.

The beam is thrust behind his neck. His arms are bound to the wood with cords, Iron nails are driven through his hands.

He is lifted up for all to see. The cross is dropped into a socket. The crowd sends up a cheer.

Two others are also being executed. Friends of Barabbas – the one who got away. They spit and curse and scream.

Now is the acid test for Jesus. He has said so much about loving enemies, blessing persecutors, turning the other cheek. Now he shows it can be done. He turns his pain to prayer:

'Forgive them, Father! They don't know what they are doing.'

The soldiers settle for the long wait. Death, when it comes, will be from hunger and thirst, exposure and exhaustion. It may take some days. Maybe a week. They gamble to pass the time – throwing dice for dead

men's clothes. Every job has its perks.
Jesus is now unrecognizable. A
writhing mass of blood and sweat. His
only cover – a blanket of flies. The
most beautiful life ever seen, hung up
in the sun like a side of meat.

Do we say 'Poor Jesus'? We should say
'Poor us'! It is our sin that has put him
there. The pain of the nails is nothing,
compared with the weight of our sin.
The taunts of the crowd are
nothing, compared with the agony of
men without God.

The Jewish leaders stroll up to inspect
their handiwork. 'Some Messiah
you've turned out to be! Get out of
that one!'
The soldiers pass the bottle. 'A little
wine, Your Majesty?'
Pilate sends a notice to be pinned

over Jesus. **'This is the King of the
Jews'.** The Roman Governor has the
last laugh. So much for the Jews!
Meanwhile, the victims talk among
themselves. One of them shouts
across to Jesus: **'Aren't you the
Messiah? Save yourself and us!'**

But the other replies: 'You're
wrong! We're getting what we
deserve. But he's done nothing.'
Then the second man calls out:
**'Remember me, Jesus, when you come
as King!'**
Jesus gives him a firm, warm
promise. **'Today you will be in
Paradise with me. We'll walk at
peace in the garden of heaven.'**

Even on the cross, Jesus has power.
Power to do what only God can do.
Power to save sinners.

The way out

23.44-49

**It was about twelve o'clock when the
sun stopped shining and darkness
covered the whole country until three
o'clock ...**

The sun hides. The light thickens.
For three hours, nature holds her
breath. In the Temple, Passover is
beginning. Thousands of lambs are
about to be killed.
The sacred trumpets blow. The
High Priest ascends the steps. It is
three o'clock. Outside the city the
perfect high priest offers the perfect
sacrifice. The Lamb of God lays down
his own life.

Jesus dies with a prayer. A prayer
from the psalms. An evening prayer:

'Father! In your hands I place my spirit!'

His death takes everyone by surprise.
It's almost as if he is ready and
willing. Almost as if he is in control.
Back in the Temple, the great
curtain hiding the Holy of Holies is
ripped from top to bottom. The
congregation gasps in horror. 'The
Holy of Holies! The place of the
Presence of God! The place where
only the High Priest goes, and then
only once a year ...
From now on the priests, the
sacrifices, and the Temple itself are
things of the past. Men and women

can come to God another way. The death of Jesus has torn down all the barriers. God's way out is man's way in.

Outside the city the crowd is beginning to disperse. Suddenly they realize what they've done. They are appalled and ashamed. They have seen many deaths, but this one is different. The army officer sums up their feelings: **'Certainly he was a good man!'**

Judge, officer, and fellow-victim all agree. Jesus was innocent.

A friend in deed

23·50-56

There was a man named Joseph, from Arimathea, a town in Judaea. He was a good and honourable man ...

Jesus must be buried before nightfall and it is already dusk. If the soldiers take him down from the cross, they'll throw him without ceremony in an unmarked grave.

Joseph has been in torment all day. A member of the Council, he has disagreed with everything that has been said and done. Now, at last, he finds his courage. He goes to Pilate and asks for the body of Jesus. He offers his own brand-new rock tomb. And Pilate agrees.

The faithful women go with Joseph. They see the body laid to rest. A boulder is rolled across the mouth of the cave to keep out thieves and animals.

Finally, they start to prepare spices and ointments to embalm the corpse. But they're too late. Everything must stop for the Sabbath. No more can be done until Sunday.

Missing

24·1-12

Very early on Sunday morning the women went to the tomb, carrying the spices they had prepared. They found the stone rolled away from the entrance to the tomb ...

The women come to the tomb at first light. They find the boulder rolled aside and the body gone!

They are astonished. It doesn't make sense. There's no mistaking the tomb. They all saw it for themselves on Friday. There's no mistaking the stone ledge and the winding sheet. They were there when the corpse was laid out.

The body of Jesus must have been stolen! But by whom? And why? Suddenly two messengers appear. Men whose clothes shine with heavenly glory. The women shrink back and bow to the ground. 'If you're looking for Jesus, you've come to the wrong place! This is a grave. But he's **alive!**'

The angels remind the women. Jesus had always said he would be raised on the third day. Slowly the news sinks in. A flicker of faith begins to warm their hearts. Of course, they remember Jesus saying such things, but they never thought for a moment that ...

They run to tell the disciples.

The Eleven aren't so easily taken in. To a man, they agree that the women are raving. Mary of Magdala has always been highly-strung. The rest are suffering from grief and wishful thinking. But something tells Peter to see for himself. And, in spite of his verdict on the women, he runs all the way!

Sure enough, the tomb is empty. The grave-clothes are still there, undisturbed! But the body itself has gone ...

Simon Peter turns for home, a very puzzled man.

12
THE
BEGINNING

Jesus is alive.
And more than alive.
He is risen!
And as for the disciples –
their story has only just begun.

It all fits!

24·13-32

On that same day two of Jesus' followers were going to a village named Emmaus, about eleven kilometres from Jerusalem ...

It's getting late. Sunset is in their eyes – and in their hearts.

Cleopas and his friend talk as they go. 'Who would have thought it? All our hopes on Jesus – and he ends up dead.'

Another traveller joins them. 'What's the great debate between you?'

Cleopas can't believe his ears! After all, what else is there to talk about? 'Have you been asleep all weekend? Haven't you heard Jesus is dead? And women have been seeing angels!'

The stranger sighs. '**How foolish you are! How slow to believe! Can't you see? It all fits!'**

The stranger begins at the beginning. He leads them step by step through Scripture. He talks about Moses and David, the Psalms and the Prophets.

'You expected a conquering king. You expected a suffering servant. But you thought the two were different. In fact they are the **same**. The Messiah **is** the suffering servant. The suffering servant **is** the Messiah!'

As they listen they forget their hot feet, their tired minds, their broken hearts. It all fits!

When they reach the village, they ask the stranger to stay.

Later, at table, he takes the bread and thanks the Father. He breaks it ... That voice! Those wounded hands ... And with that he is gone!

The same Jesus

24·33-49

They got up at once and went back to Jerusalem, where they found the eleven disciples gathered together with the others and saying, 'The Lord is risen indeed! He has appeared to Simon!'

While the two were telling them this, suddenly the Lord himself stood among them and said to them, 'Peace be with you.'

It's the same Jesus.

They shrink from him, thinking he's a ghost. But ghosts don't eat. He shows his hands and feet, wickedly scarred. Can it be ...?

And then he starts to teach ... The gentleness. The quiet truth. The catchy joy of life. Now there's no doubt. It's him!

He doesn't go to Pilate or the Council to set the record straight. He doesn't descend on the guard room to put them right and pay them back.

Instead he comes softly to his friends. And gives them peace.

It's the same Jesus.
So why don't they recognize him? Because he's **different!** When last they saw him he was hanging high. A mutilated mess oozing blood. Every bone and muscle and nerve silently screaming. Now he's different.
He's alive. And more than alive. He is risen!
He's gone on. He's gone through. He's in another world.
Heaven.

Glory!

24.50-53

Then he led them out of the city as far as Bethany, where he raised his hands and blessed them. As he was blessing them, he departed from them and was taken up into heaven. They worshipped him and went back into Jerusalem, filled with great joy, and spent all their time in the Temple giving thanks to God.

Jesus returns to his Father.
He has blazed the trail. He has built the bridge. The way out is complete.
Son of Man, Son of God, he takes his place in glory. And as he does so, he draws our world with him into his.